TWISTED FABLES
FOR TWISTED MINDS

TWISTED FABLES
FOR TWISTED MINDS

BAREFOOT DOCTOR

This will either heal you
or make you go insane

Element
An Imprint of HarperCollins*Publishers*
77–85 Fulham Palace Road,
Hammersmith, London W6 8JB

The website address is: www.thorsonselement.com

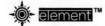

and *Element* are trademarks of
HarperCollins*Publishers* Ltd

First published by Element in 2003

1 3 5 7 9 10 8 6 4 2

© Barefoot Doctor, Stephen Russell 2003

Stephen Russell asserts the moral right to
be identified as the author of this work

A catalogue record of this book
is available from the British Library

ISBN 0 00 716485 8

Printed and bound in Great Britain by
Clays Ltd, St Ives plc

For Jake

FOREWORD

by Dr Squid Gridlo, Philosopher

When first approached by Barefoot Doctor to write the foreword to this collection of fables, on account of his reputation I was, of course, flattered.

On the initial read-through I was amused and bewildered.

On the second run-through, although I still had some mild feelings of queasiness and disorientation, I was starting to wonder if there wasn't perhaps something in what he was saying.

By the third time round, I was forced to admit, bemusedly, that this collection of loosely-woven histories of a group of highly bizarre individuals was in fact of the utmost profundity and importance to the world.

What initially appeared as utter nonsense, suddenly came alive to me as a living metaphor for the absolute absurdity of the so-called real-life stories of the countless people I have had the privilege of drawing into conversation, during the course of my extensive travels on this crazy planet.

Though not being given naturally to contemplating matters of the spirit, being more of a pragmatist by disposition, I found myself being transformed incrementally and exponentially with each passing parable by the certain knowledge of one thing, which finds its exegesis so eloquently facilitated in these pages.

This, namely, that the only constant factor in all known existence is change. Furthermore, that change is unpredictable by nature. It is only in the acceptance of being in the state of not knowing what comes next, that one finds enlightenment and hence joy in the absolutely unfathomable mystery of life and death.

These fables, each allegedly based faithfully on snippets of true occurrences, all cut and pasted anarchically together, will at first seem totally unbelievable. That is for sure. However, when you stop for a moment to reflect on the truly ridiculous stories of those you meet along the way as you wander this great thoroughfare of life, you may well begin to wonder who's the more crazy: you, or Barefoot Doctor.

In the end, you'll probably agree with me that we're all of us inmates in this loony bin we've created here on Earth, and it is for this precise reason I am proud to provide this foreword to what can only be described as a totally insane text, and hope you derive as much pleasure and benefit from it as I have.

Dr Squid Gridlo, Lucerne, Switzerland 2003

AUTHOR'S BRIEF INTRODUCTION

Twisted Fables for Twisted Minds is an unlikely expedition into the deeper realms of the human psyche. It deals radically with the theme of quantum personal transformation, something occurring with greater and greater frequency and intensity in people's lives at this time, as the thrust for evolution accelerates against a backdrop of impending catastrophe.

In this book I use the age-old teaching device of distracting your thinking mind through the telling of fables (always stronger in impact on your psyche than fact), causing you to enter a mild, childlike trance state wherein you find yourself quite happy to suspend critical judgement just long enough (for a barefoot doctor) to pop a series of nuggets of potentially precious transformative data into your personal circuitry, which will contribute immediately (it is hoped) to your spiritual, mental, emotional, physical and material well-being, in a far more efficacious way than would happen if you simply read a straight-ahead self-help manual.

Read the fables as twisted fiction with a moral, or read them as entertaining self-help, it doesn't matter – either way you risk profoundly disturbing the status quo of your mind, but nothing worthwhile ever occurs in this life without a bit of disturbance preceding it and the personal pay off could be huge – for both of us.

Of course some of the characters you'll relate to, some you won't. By the same token, some of them won't relate to you either, but that's life and let's not get silly about this – the important thing is that when you recognize yourself in any of the characters, you learn to love yourself, or at least like yourself more as a result.

These fables are inspired by the 'miracle' of healing that comes to every life at the most unexpected moments and in the most unlikely ways. May it come to you at precisely the moments you need it most, in the ways that suit you best, and may all limitations to your perfect peace, fulfillment, moment-to-moment satisfaction and contentment, whether self-imposed or apparently otherwise, be instantaneously and incrementally removed with every passing word.

Barefoot Doctor, Eastern Catalunya, 2003

WARNING: This is self-help as you've never seen it before – it may give rise to uncontrollable random bouts of existential levity. Not to be used while driving, cycling or operating heavy machinery. Not to be taken internally. If in doubt, seek medical advice. Always read with care!

This will either heal you or make you go insane.

1

Brandell Willard, a lost young man with large ears and unruly features, was about to top himself. Everything was going wrong in his life. Just as he was going to leap off Suicide Bridge, a being (maybe an angel, maybe a barefoot doctor), grabbed his arm.

'Stop young fella. Reality as you experience it, is an illusion, a trick of the light, merely a series of impressions you're holding on to. If it's too painful, simply change your perception and you will change the very nature and structure of reality itself.'

'It's not reality that messes me up,' replied Brandell, 'it's other people letting me down. How can I change other people?'

'You can't, but you can change the energy you're putting out, which in turn will change the way people treat you. That's the Wayward Taoist approach,' replied the kindly being.

Brandell heard all this but jumped anyway – stupid sod.

If you want to make a change in your life, try this: As you breathe in, gather up the essence of all the doubt, worry, anxiety and negativity within you. As you breathe out, expel that existential dross from yourself. As you breathe in again, let in the new good coming your way, which will appear for you right now in an appropriate mix of warmth, abundance, colour and light.

2

Lango Faldo was dark, handsome, symmetrical of feature, rugged and lean but he had no money. He believed it was a virtue to be poor. He believed there was only a finite supply of wealth and that if he had some, he'd be depriving someone else. So he lived alone in a darkened room feeling miserable.

One day, in a dream, he was visited by a being (maybe an angel, maybe a barefoot doctor), who whispered, 'You've got it all wrong buddy. There's nothing virtuous about poverty. Poverty sucks. There is an infinite supply of wealth – money is only energy in disguise, hence why it's called currency – it flows like a river through society. All you have to do is divert that flow your way.'

'How?' asked Lango, suddenly becoming interested.

'Picture yourself sitting up against your favourite tree. Look up and notice the leaves are banknotes. As you continue to watch, the leaves start dropping on the ground all around you. Scoop up a few grand and put it in your pocket. Come back every day – the supply is inexhaustible. Do this for a week and before you know it, you'll be rich, young man.'

Lango Faldo woke from his dream and, remembering, did the money tree visualization. Would you believe it, three days later an old woman he'd been kind to once left him twenty-three million pounds in her will.

Lango Faldo moved to a big house on the hill, lived in the lap of luxury and became a total arsehole.

If your relationship with money isn't all it could be or you'd simply like more, try the money tree visualization for yourself. Just remember to retain your modesty, humility and compassion for those less fortunate than you when it works.

3

Sitting in his mansion on the hill, Lango Faldo realized his new-found friends were merely fair-weather while his old friends could no longer relate to him.

He felt a gnawing void within that no amount of alcohol, drugs, sex or partying could assuage. When Dallalia Wilkins, petite New Age con artiste with a small but sexy mouth, walked into his life, he was ripe for the picking.

By investing his money in her so-called spiritual pyramid sales scheme, she said, he'd once again find meaning in his life.

But seven months later found him a broken man, sleeping rough near Charing Cross. One night, a being (maybe an angel, maybe a barefoot doctor), stopped and bunged him a euro.

'It's all just the play of yin and yang,' he said.

In that moment, Lango became enlightened.

He realized it was love that makes the world go round, not money.

He started wandering the world, spreading the word, amassing many followers. Journalists started writing about him in glowing terms, linking him to this celebrity and that; people posted messages about him and his wondrous powers in chat rooms far and wide; he got into running workshops about how to love one another, started coining it in and had soon made a million.

If you want to generate that kind of magic in your life right now, start at once by visualizing a stream of crimson-coloured light emanating from your chest and enveloping the world with love.

Dallalia Wilkins, petite New Age con artiste with a small but sexy mouth, who had taken Lango Faldo for everything he had with her so-called spiritual, crooked pyramid sales venture, developed a vicious coke habit and ended up in rehab.

One night, in a dream, she was visited by a being (maybe an angel, maybe a barefoot doctor), who said, 'Listen honey, if you go around conning people, you'll denude your life of authenticity. Without that it doesn't matter how much money or how many guys you have, you'll always be tormented. Use that talent you have for gaining peoples' confidence to heal them instead.'

'But how?' she asked.

All she remembered then was a blinding flash of light enter through the back of her head, jolting her awake.

Three years later, the walls of her treatment room now lined with certificates for crystal healing, aromatherapy, metamorphic reflexology and Sicilian energy pulsing, her hands, which had once been moisturized, manicured and bejeweled, now those of an honest working woman (or just about), she got up from her bureau where she was idly flicking through a deck of tarot cards to answer a knock at the door.

Lango Faldo, now world-famous spiritual teacher, thought he'd mastered his anger, thought he'd just walk in and say thank you for the lesson that had eventually led to his genuinely good fortune, thought he'd be filled with enlightened compassion, thought he'd simply forgive her.

But one look at that face, something inside him snapped and he bopped her one, hard on the nose.

Anger arises from fire in the liver. If you want to handle your anger towards someone, take a deep breath and make the sound sssshhhhhh. Mentally see your liver cooling down. Then in your mind and heart say to that person: 'I forgive you. I no longer seek revenge.'

5

Brandell Willard, the stupid sod who'd jumped off Suicide Bridge, did not die. He landed on a bouncy castle on a passing fairground truck headed for Aberdeen.

On arrival, he dusted himself off, made for the nearest New Age encampment and enrolled on a loving relationships training programme led by a certain Professo Expressional, who candidly said, 'This stuff's never going to work for you, son, you're just too damn ugly to find a woman.'

For the second time in his young life, Brandell gave up. He went to the beach, took a slug of vodka, one temazapam and 50ml of ketamin, then gaffer-taped a plastic bag over his head, looked out to the cold North Sea and waited to die.

Just then, a being appeared (maybe an angel, maybe a barefoot doctor), who said, 'Listen kid, you're ugly because you've lost your inner light. Take that bag off your head and breathe the light of the world into your heart. Fill your chest with that light and the beauty of it will animate your features and make you irresistible.'

Brandell didn't hear him, however, because the bag muffled the sound. But just as his chest was about to burst, he developed a vicious itch on the crown of his head, worse than the bites from a thousand mosquitoes working in concert.

He ripped the bag off to scratch his head and as he did, his chest was flooded with love. He forgave the world, himself, his mother, his father, his siblings, his schoolteachers, even the bully at school, and strode off into town.

Dallalia Wilkins, petite ex-New Age con artiste turned healer, recently punched on the nose by Lango Faldo, the famous spiritual teacher she'd fleeced, looked up from her green tea as Brandell passed by the café and fell instantly, insanely in love.

Don't dwell in despondency. Take the light of the world into your chest as you breathe in. Breathe out and let your inner beauty radiate for everyone to enjoy.

6

Salbinellas Marina, psychic counsellor, lying in bed next to Professo Expressional (she'd met him at one of his loving relationships trainings in Aberdeen) said, 'That boy you told was too ugly to find a woman, who tried to kill himself on the beach ...'

'Manic depressive,' Professo interjected.

'... Well, I think you've got a problem with compassion. Would you be willing to see a friend of mine? I think he could help you.'

'Who?'

'Lango Faldo, the world famous spiritual teacher.'

'That charlatan!'

'You're just being insecure. Faldo's for real. You, on the other hand, have a distinct air of inauthenticity and that's why the sex is getting boring.'

Expressional looked down sheepishly at his flaccid genitalia. 'OK, I'll go.'

Lango Faldo had met his type before. Pompous, arrogant know-it-alls, running trainings in subjects they screw up on in their own lives. Loving relationships! This monkey couldn't love his way out of a cereal packet, Faldo mused.

'To gain authenticity, you have to be yourself, not who you think you are or should be,' Faldo informed him.

Trouble was, Expressional didn't know how to do that. He grew depressed, went into a decline, revisited a previous crack habit and during one session suffered a minor heart attack. For that moment while he left his body, he was met by a being (maybe an angel, maybe a barefoot doctor) who said, 'Breathe!' That was all, but in that instant Professo was enlightened. He snapped back into his body, realizing that if nothing else, the breath is real and all he had to do to be himself was breathe.

Lying in bed the next day, he turned to Salbinellas with her honey-blond hair cascading over her graceful shoulders. His manhood was now hard and swollen, but her mind was elsewhere. She was thinking of Lango and the way his hands moved when he spoke.

Be yourself. Do it with love. Start by becoming aware of your breathing. Put your palm on your solar plexus (upper abdomen) and make sure your diaphragm is relaxed, especially when talking on the phone, at meetings, wherever or whatever.

7

Lango Faldo, world famous spiritual teacher, contemplated his hands and thought about Salbinellas Marina – the way her honey-blond hair cascaded over her graceful shoulders – and wondered how she could be interested in that chump Expressional.

It had been a while since he'd punched petite New Age con artiste Dallalia Wilkins on the nose for ripping him off and he was finally over her.

Being enlightened now, he thought he'd be free of his desire for women, but Salbinellas Marina really blew his hair back. He simply had to have her. His desire overrode his conscience and he picked up the phone.

'I'm glad you called,' she said warmly, 'I've been thinking about you.'

'Funny that, I've been thinking of you too. Do you want to come over?'

Two days later, they were still in bed and so

engrossed in each other that they didn't hear when the doorbell rang.

When no one answered, Professo Expressional walked round the side of the building, peered in through the slats of the venetian blinds, caught a glimpse of Wilkins' naked legs and honey-blond hair amongst the rumpled bedclothes, and began crying like a baby until he was no more than a blubbering heap in the alleyway. He stumbled out onto the street and collapsed on the pavement.

Just then, a being (maybe an angel, maybe a barefoot doctor) passed by and said, 'Hey Mac, the Tao expresses itself through many forms, not just that one. No one's indispensable, you know what I'm saying? There're plenty more fish in the air.'

'Don't you mean sea?'

'Sea, air, what's the difference? Pick yourself up and dust yourself off. Go into town and look for the Tao in every woman you meet. One door closes, a better one opens, you dig what I'm saying?'

But Expressional didn't hear him. He was watching tantalized as Dallalia Wilkins rushed by, shouting imploringly, 'But why don't you want me?' at that odd-looking young man with large ears from the training, who seemed to be trying to get away from her ....

Consider whose form you might be clinging to. Sink your consciousness backwards into the centre of your brain, into the endless expanse of inner space synonymous with the Tao itself and, holding the image of that person steady before you, let your inner eye spy the Tao within them too. As you do this say: 'I release you,' three times. Then see them turn around and go. If they're really meant for you they'll come back to you of their own accord. Say with gentle conviction until you mean it: 'What's for me won't pass me by and what passes me by wasn't for me.'

8

Across the half-empty bar, Rits Historìco, notorious underworld figure smelling richly of expensive Milanese cologne, noticed the desperate young man nursing his bourbon.

Brandell Willard thought he might go insane. The loneliness that had driven him twice to attempt suicide had now turned to frightened despair. That crazy, small-mouthed, broken-nosed obsessive, Dallalia Wilkins, had her hooks into him and he was running scared.

When Historìco approached him with a proposal that involved helping him shift a ton of smack into Texas, he jumped at the opportunity to escape.

He shipped the consignment easily enough, ingeniously disguising it as bathroom cleaner, and with his considerable profit bought a secluded villa on the Spanish Costa Del Sol. There he fell in with the local underworld and perpetrated a few minor dodgy deals, including some with Rits, who, fearing Willard was getting too big for his boots, grassed him up to the police.

Lying anguished beneath the incessant glare of the overhead naked bulb, his newfound fortune lost, Brandell listened to the warden's footsteps going back and forth all night outside his cell. Falling into a spontaneous trance, he felt he was communing with a being (maybe an angel, maybe a barefoot doctor), who said, 'You've come a long way since Suicide Bridge, kid.'

'Yeah, but this looks like the end of the road for me,' replied the disillusioned young Willard.

'Balderdash!' replied the being, 'There's no obstacle between heaven and earth you can't surmount if you believe in yourself enough.' At which he placed his hands on Brandell's head, infused something invisible and disappeared.

Just then, an unprecedented 7.2 earthquake ripped the Andalucian jail asunder. Wasting no time, Brandell made a run for it through a gaping hole in the wall and arrived at the Portuguese border by nightfall, sporting a false walrus moustache.

If you feel blocked by a seemingly insurmountable obstacle, repeat the following affirmation till you mean it: 'I am the king or queen of No Matter What. There are no obstacles to my perfect fulfillment.' As you believe, so will it be.

9

Professo Expressional, loving relationships trainer and intermittent crack addict, recently left by Salbinellas Marina for Lango Faldo, world-famous spiritual teacher, couldn't get Dallalia Wilkins, petite ex-New Age con artiste turned healer and her small but sexy mouth, out of his mind.

He followed her to her new clinic in Miami, phoning his agent first to set up a seminar there so he could claim the trip as a business expense, and made an appointment for a treatment with her for the day after the seminar.

However the loving relationships training went down so well – people there being more earnest about such things – that he instantly became a local star and settled down to a life of ease on the Florida Keys, soon forgetting all about Dallalia, and even forgetting to send her the cancellation fee for the treatment.

One night, spurred on by tropical ennui, he

fell into an impromptu crack session with a group of Jamaican construction workers, during which he went into an extraordinary altered state, started hearing strange voices and ended up being sectioned by the Florida State Mental Health Department.

Through his befuddled, sedated haze, he thought he saw a being (maybe an angel, maybe a barefoot doctor), saying, 'You're alive!'

This simple yet profound statement, sometimes used by regression therapists when they can't 'pull' the patient back into the present, rocked Expressional to his core. He snapped to, and on securing his own release, started going to NA meetings and got heavily into religion.

Never fight shy of the adventure on offer. Always follow your fascination, for in your fascination will you find your true life story. Repeat this affirmation till you mean it: 'I no longer need hold back from living out the fullest or wildest adventure on offer to me. By following my fascination and overriding my fear, I find my purpose and fulfillment.'

10

Salbinellas Marina knew how to use her sexual charms and was used to getting her way with wealthy men.

Lango Faldo, world-famous spiritual teacher, was aware he had a pattern of being taken for his money by attractive women and was on his guard.

He pondered the crown of her head, with her honey-blond hair cascading over her graceful shoulders, as it bobbed gently up and down in his naked lap and brought her to rest with his hand.

'What's up?' she asked, looking up surprised.

'I feel insecure,' Lango replied.

'Why, what's bothering you?' she pressed.

'You seem to be the kind of girl who's attracted to a man's money rather than his soul. How do I know if it's me or my money you're after?'

'Stupid, it's you I love, not your money,' she replied.

'Why?'

'It's your hands.'

Faldo, mollified, distractedly looked at his hands, one either side of her head, and half-consciously re-instigated the bobbing motion, leaning back as the pleasure overtook him, then took her to town and bought her a bracelet for €9000. Later, Salbinellas smiled coyly to herself in the bathroom mirror.

That night, Lango had a dreadful nightmare, wherein a being (maybe an angel, maybe a bare-foot doctor) said, 'All your worldly possessions are about to leave you for a second time, Faldo. Do not be dismayed, however. It is only to teach you more about non-attachment – all part of the job of being an enlightened master.'

Faldo awoke in a sweat to find Salbinellas gone, along with his car keys, credit cards, cash and the deeds to his international property portfolio.

Don't be dismayed by the coming and going of things or people. It's all just grist for the mill of your enlightenment process. Don't hold on – let them go to make way for the new. Visualize an endless stream of abundance that's there you to enjoy, entering through your navel like a stream of golden light as you breathe in, filling your entire being and radiating through your chest for others to enjoy as you breathe out. In this very moment you have everything you need. Trust that.

11

When Brandell Willard's help-me letter, written one day in desperation from Portugal, arrived special delivery at the new natural health clinic in Miami that Dallalia Wilkins had opened to take advantage of the older demographic there, she instantly dropped everything, including the elderly lady's head she was holding, onto the treatment couch and made straight for Tavira, the small Algarve fishing village where Brandell, recently, miraculously, escaped from an Andalucian gaol, was serving behind a bar, not recognizing him at first on account of his false walrus moustache.

She agreed to set him up as clinic manager, install him in her luxury home and lend him $23,000 tide-over money and for the first time he noticed how attractive she was.

Seven months later he'd vanished. Her home, her clinic and all her money had gone on financing a large consignment of cocaine from Colombia on his behalf. Dallalia wound up on the street, homeless and destitute in New Mexico, where one night, as if from a distant star, a being appeared (maybe an angel, maybe a barefoot doctor), who said, 'You are experiencing nothing more than the workings of the law of cause and effect. If you want to change your karma, do something to help.'

Just then, a disenfranchised and heavily inebriated Native American was about to step out in front of a speeding, off-road sports utility vehicle. Dallalia managed to grab his arm in the nick of time and save his life. As she did, she spotted an expensive Italian attaché case under a parked car. She slipped down a side street and, kicking open the locks, blinked in awe as she counted six million Swiss Francs in unused banknotes and a fish paste sandwich.

If you feel like your karma's stuck on account of some previous misdeed you haven't remembered to forgive yourself for, go immediately and help someone who needs it. Then forgive yourself with the help of the following affirmation, to be repeated till you mean it: 'I forgive myself.'

12

Professo Expressional, ex-loving relationships trainer, who'd found religion as a substitute for his occasional crack addiction and become an ordained minister and preacher of a minor but radical Southern Baptist church, had had it with Alabama. He threw some stuff in a suitcase, threw the suitcase in his old Oldsmobile and drove to Manhattan.

He was disillusioned. Even with all his religion, his existential angst was starting to burst through the fragile seams of his psyche. He wasn't paying attention to the road when he smashed head first into an oncoming retro-rock band tour bus. As his head rammed into the fortunately sturdy windshield and he lost consciousness, he heard a being (maybe an angel, maybe a barefoot doctor) whispering to him, as if from another dimension, 'Pssst, Professo, Professo, you're disillusioned because it's hard to find the god you're looking for in all that religious baloney you've been preaching, or in a lungful of crack, for that matter. You won't even find it in a woman. The god you're looking for can only be accessed in your own heart.'

When Expressional finally came to in intensive care, suffering from amnesia, he didn't remember anything: neither the crash, the being, nor the religion. He felt like a new person altogether. Realizing all at once that his innate sexual drive was an unconscious, instinctive urge to not only meld with womankind, but to actually join it, as soon as he was able, he went straight to northern California, had a not too painful sex change, and entered holy orders as an unremarkable-looking Buddhist nun called Sister Kimbal Neosho.

If you feel disillusioned and existential unrest is disturbing your peace of mind, spend some time talking informally to the spiritual presence that resides in your heart. Visualize yourself in a perfected state about eight cm tall, sitting cross-legged like a miniature Buddha in the centre of your chest and ask this little Buddha to reveal what wants changing in your own life.

13

Lango Faldo, one-time world famous spiritual teacher, twice relieved of all worldly possessions by beguiling female opportunists, was now making a go of it as a personal fitness trainer and was off to do his first session with Rits Historìco, notorious underworld figure, at Rits's Belgravia penthouse.

As Rits went through his free-weights paces, he turned to Faldo and said, 'Say, haven't I seen you somewhere before? Wait a minute, weren't you that world-famous spiritual teacher?'

'I was, but ...'

'What happened, couldn't make it pay?'

'No, it paid alright. I got fleeced of all my money. Twice.'

'Who by?'

'First time by Dallalia Wilkins ...'

'Oh, yeah, the petite New-Age con artiste who struck it rich and became a healer. And the second time?'

'By Salbinellas Mar ...' Just then, Salbinellas Marina sauntered in, her honey-blond hair cascading over her graceful shoulders, wearing a French maid's outfit. 'Time for our little afternoon game,' she said, pouting at Historìco, unaware of Lango's presence.

Rits, thinking on his feet, pressed a hidden button and a large, psychopathic-looking man dressed in an Italian black suit and black polo neck appeared in the doorway. 'Capstan, bump this chump off, he may cause trouble', Rits instructed, pointing at Faldo.

Faldo did not even stop to shoot Salbinellas a recriminating look. He made straight for the window and, crashing through it blind, landed on the roof of an adjacent building, bolted down a fire escape and lost himself in the incongruous afternoon crowd on Sloane Street. With Capstan hard at heel he hid in a doorway of a department store till the danger had passed, then sat down on a step and wept.

Just then, a being strolled by (maybe an angel, maybe a barefoot doctor), tossed him a euro and said, 'Say, haven't I seen you somewhere before? Look buddy, don't waste time lamenting what could have been, or you'll miss any new opportunity coming your way.'

When Lango's eyes had cleared, the being was gone, but on the step was a newspaper. Lango picked it up, read a job ad, phoned the number and became a prime-time TV presenter.

If you're lamenting lost opportunities, stop and repeat this affirmation till you mean it: 'I now pluck a new opportunity out of thin air, like ripe fruit from a tree.'

14

Porphyry Trents, bigwig in Scottish politics who looked damn fetching in a suit and heels, was so inspired by watching Lango Faldo – one-time world-famous spiritual teacher, ex-personal fitness trainer, now TV personality – present his prime-time family entertainment show that she jacked in her high-level job in order to live her life's dream. She set off for Hoxton in east London at once, where she studied flying trapeze, went for the triple somersault, and cracked her spine in three places.

As she lay on the mat, squealing in agony, wondering who she could sue, a being (maybe an angel, maybe a barefoot doctor) appeared through the mists of her pain. He passed his hands over the breaks and said (to that part of Porphyry that was, is and will always be whole), 'If you choose it, you can heal that back of yours.'

In that moment, Porphyry Trents instantly saw through the illusory nature of physical existence, started to laugh out loud and to the astonishment of the ambulance men, stood up.

As she did, however, her local mind, little Porphyry Trents, said inside her head, 'Look at me, I've cracked my spine in three places and just because some random being tells me I can heal myself, I'm up and walking. How fantastic!' At which she suddenly crumpled into a oddly shaped heap on the floor, and screamed.

Her spine did in fact heal, much to the amazement of the cynical medical doctors, and she returned to the trapeze. A while later she was spotted doing the triple at a festival and whisked off to Hollywood to feature in a circus movie. She became a star and eventually wound up as a bigwig in American politics instead.

Never doubt your power to heal other people or yourself. Always address that part of others or yourself which has always been healed or whole and will always be so, no matter what. The physical healing will follow on naturally some time after. Visualize yourself in a state of perfect wholeness right now, all disease and pain banished. Then take a deep breath and say: 'Thank you.'

15

When HT Russell – the floppy-haired retro-rock band whose tour bus had collided with the Oldsmobile driven by Professo Expressional – one-time loving-relationships trainer and ex-preacher, who'd subsequently undergone a sex change and become Sister Kimbal Neosho, Buddhist nun – wanted to hold a concert on a platform suspended by ropes and pulleys between two downtown Manhattan skyscrapers, 1010 feet up in mid-air, precise location to be kept secret till the day for obvious reasons, they knew there was only one person who could arrange it for them: Senator Porphyry Trents of New York.

After much deliberation, Trents, dressed for effect in dark suit and heels, looked up from her massive rosewood and chrome desk at each member of HT Russell in turn and said, 'My lover likes your music, she's a real fan. For that reason, I'm going to give you clearance.' And with some misgivings she bade them all farewell.

On the day of the concert, with the upturned faces of all Manhattan gathered in the streets and squares of SoHo and the Village below, just as H, the skinny guitarist, jacked up the level on his digital psychedelic effects unit, a freak electrical storm blew in off the Atlantic, a bolt of lightning burned clean through the ropes and the platform supporting HT Russell started dropping in a fierce and furious 1010 ft descent.

The band stopped playing almost immediately and began to scream, but realizing they were now unplugged and inaudible, soon became deathly silent as they hurtled to the ground. Just then, a being (maybe an angel, maybe a barefoot doctor), appeared as if from nowhere and said something. But no one knows what because they all died on impact, except the drummer who was still playing to the click track in his headphones and died four bars later.

Always be willing to die living a great adventure rather than spending the rest of your time hiding in life's cul-de-sacs. Meanwhile, if you're always two steps behind the action, take your metaphorical headphones off and repeat this affirmation till you mean it: 'I am always in the right place at the right time doing the right thing with the right result.'

16

When Dallalia Wilkins – petite one-time New Age con artiste turned ex-healer, fleeced of all her money and possessions by young Brandell Willard, one-time suicidal depressive turned drug-mule then con man – found an attaché case containing six million Swiss francs and a fish paste sandwich under a parked car in New Mexico, she immediately threw the sandwich away and invested the money in a live multi-media comedy show in Barcelona. This did so well she wasted no time investing in a high-risk off-Broadway show that went on to Broadway in no time at all and broke all box-office records that month.

Dallalia was up with the New York City interior design craze for ex-Russian fighter plane ejector seats. She had one in her Chelsea office high above Eighth Avenue.

Why she tampered with the don't-press-this button, nobody knows, but as she went crashing through the sealed glass window into empty space beyond and was on the verge of a major coronary, a being appeared out of nowhere (maybe an angel, maybe just a barefoot doctor), who shouted, 'Never lose your faith, it's always worked out fine up until now,' and then vanished back to wherever he came from.

How stupid, she thought, and prepared for the worst, but the weather was with her and a strong gust of westerly wind altered her trajectory and sent her hurtling onto Brandell Willard, who was tugging his earlobe, lost in thought, counting the piles of rubber stock he kept on the roof of his Seventh Avenue light industrial unit where, unbeknownst to her, he'd been producing mass-market rubber and fetish wear, thereby breaking both his legs.

Next time you're in a mild or strong panic, don't think of ejecting – instead slow down your breath, press the centre of your palm quite hard for 59 seconds and repeat 'I can do it' till you mean it. Thing's will either work out (or they won't). Why panic?

17

When Lango Faldo, one-time world-famous spiritual teacher, ex-personal fitness trainer turned prime-time family entertainment terrestrial TV presenter, heard that Rits Historìco, notorious underworld character, was still after him for threatening to expose Rits' girl, Salbinellas Marina, as an opportunist and con woman, he took it as a sign to lie low for a while. His series had just come to an end anyway and it would be some weeks at least before the TV channel decided if they wanted it re-commissioned.

He packed a small bag and set off for northern California, where on the spur of the moment he checked in at a so-called spiritual retreat run by Sister Kimbal Neosho, unremarkable-looking Buddhist nun, who prior to her sex-change had been (bearded, monocle-wearing) Professo Expressional, ex-loving relationships trainer and occasional crack addict turned preacher, who'd taken holy orders to escape his inner turmoil.

Neosho was startled to see Faldo here. All at once, she remembered him telling her, (when she was still Expressional), 'Be yourself, not who you think you are.' She stopped her morning walking meditation (foot lifts, foot glides, foot plants itself and so on), sat down on a meditation rock, acknowledged to herself that her personal identity crisis was far from over and began to cry.

Through her tears she thought she saw a being (maybe an angel, maybe a barefoot doctor), who said, 'Listen baby, I ain't no shaven-headed Bodhisattva, but I'll tell you this: doesn't matter if you've got a body, haven't got a body, got a man's body or a woman's, the only thing you can ever truly identify with is the source of all being itself. Everything else is just passing form.'

When Kimbal Neosho stood up to continue with her lift-glide-and-planting, her perspective had profoundly altered and she felt reborn.

Breaking into a run, she made a bee-line for Lango's meditation cell, where he was sitting in full lotus, serenely observing the passing of breath in and out through the end of his nose, and ripping her habit off as she ran, threw herself on top of him, knocking him clean over onto the cold tiled floor.

If you're caught in an existential quandary and have forgotten who you really are, repeat this affirmation till you mean it: 'The power that creates the world is also within me. I live surrounded in its grace.' As you do this visualize the power as a column of rose-gold coloured light running up your spine and the grace as a force field of white-gold light surrounding you.

18

When Nervo Nergal – daring, dashing Brazilian Capoeira champion – heard his childhood sweetheart, Salbinellas Marinas – opportunist, con woman and girlfriend of Rits Historìco, notorious underworld character – was in town, he made straight for her hotel, skillfully dodging the Rio carnival crowds and cartwheeling deftly onto the dining terrace where she was eating with Historìco and his minder, Capstan.

As he pulled up a chair and sat down uninvited, Rits, not allowing for Latin temperament, told Capstan to, 'get rid of this joker', which seemed to press Nervo's buttons so hard he span into another cartwheel, kicking both Capstan and his boss on their respective temples simultaneously so hard they both died instantly.

'I'm coming with you!' said Salbinellas as Nervo looked right, looked left, looked right again and made to dash off down the street and lose himself in a nearby pavella until he could arrange safe passage to the north till the heat died down.

Holed up with Nervo now in a beach cabana in Bahia, Salbinellas was growing antsy. She'd learned to play berimbau, talked with the dolphins, and discovered that childhood sweethearts don't always travel so well through time. She suddenly got up, left the house, wandered into the forest, met a shaman who blew something strange down a pipe into her mouth and went into a deep trip where she was visited by a being (maybe an angel, maybe a barefoot doctor, maybe just a little green man), who said, 'My dear, your existence feels meaningless because you contribute nothing to the world. Do something with your time that will enhance things for others.'

Thirty-six hours later, as soon as the effects of the drug wore off, she went home, packed her bags and without stopping to say bye, headed straight for New York City, where she enrolled in college at once, got her broker's license and went into business selling pricey loft conversions in and around SoHo from a cellphone.

Whether you're fulfilled or not, repeat this affirmation till you feel it: 'My existence has value to the world,' then think of new ways to contribute this value that will benefit you too and set the wheels in motion without delay.

19

By the time Lango Faldo, prime-time TV star, one-time world-famous spiritual teacher and ex-personal fitness trainer, came to his senses after being knocked unconscious by sex-crazed Kimbal Neosho, unremarkable-looking Buddhist nun – once Professo Expressional, loving relationships trainer and occasional crack addict turned preacher, who had recently undergone a sex change – he had already been stripped naked and was receiving wet kisses up and down the length of his shivering, goosebumped body.

With his mind refreshed from doing nothing but observing the ingress and egress of breath for ten days, it took him no time to recognize who Neosho was or had been, and brushing her off roughly, he staggered into the bathroom to sit on the toilet and think things over quietly.

Looking down into the toilet bowl at the ripples in the water and what-have-you he discerned the face of a being (maybe an angel, maybe a bare-foot doctor), staring up at him, who said, 'This is all just happening to remind you who you really are,' and then disappeared down the S-bend.

Wasting no time, he gathered his belongings, mumbled his thank yous and leaving Neosho doing a panting (with unrequited desire) meditation on the floor, got the hell out of there and didn't stop till he reached Los Angeles. There he made straight for Hollywood, got in touch with his old press agent and in no time was back in business as a spiritual teacher to the rich and famous, making so much money he hardly batted an eyelid when he read the TV channel's email informing him they'd dropped his series in favour of one hosted by a three-and-a-half year old as part of their drive to reach younger audiences.

If someone close to you is acting in mildly off-putting ways, repeat this affirmation till you believe it: 'People act towards me the way they do to remind me who I really am and where I really want to be.'

✦

20

When Dallalia Wilkins, petite one-time New Age con artiste and ex-healer with a small but sexy mouth, now turned Broadway producer, landed in her ex-Russian fighter plane ejector seat on Brandell Willard, large-eared, unruly featured, one-time suicidal manic depressive, drugs mule and ex-con man turned New York manufacturer and distributor of mass-market rubber and fetish wear, with whom she'd been obsessed for ages, and broke both his legs, she couldn't believe her luck.

She took him to her summer house at the Hamptons to recuperate and instead of physiotherapy she paid for him to study power yoga with Placentia Ordanato, the ravishing beauty who held all of New York and London in the palm of her hand.

Brandell fell in love with Placentia at first sight and because he knew how to breathe in the light of the world to beautify his rather ugly features, she fell in love with him too. A torrid affair soon blossomed behind Dallalia's back, who in any case was too absorbed in her new Broadway hit show to notice anything askew.

But as soon as his legs were healed, Brandell sold the goodwill in his business for only a little less than $155,281, absconded with as much of Wilkins's cash as he could lay hands on and with spellbound Placentia in tow, escaped to the semi-arid desert island of Gomera to live in undisturbed exile for a while among the taciturn inhabitants of a remote fishing village, whilst opening a power yoga retreat intended to cater to stressed city trader types from London and Frankfurt.

When Dallalia came home and discovered his note, 'Gone to Gomera,' she was overcome with grief and rage. She ran to her car and driving at 80 in a 30mph zone through sleeting rain, blinded by the deathly glare of headlights, she tore back into town to see her therapist, got stuck in the elevator between the thirty-eighth and thirty-ninth floors because of a power cut and passed out from oxygen deprivation, only to have a being appear to her (maybe an angel, maybe a barefoot doctor), who said, 'Therapy won't help you now, girl. Just hold the vision of him in your mind's eye and say, "I wish you peace, my brother," three times, then let him go and find yourself a new distraction.'

'Look, do me a favour with that New Age rubbish,' she was about to reply, but the power went back on and with it the aircon. The elevator started up and so did she, running into her therapist to talk the whole thing over and then jumping on the first plane to Tenerife to get the boat to Gomera.

If there's someone you're having a hard time releasing, picture them before you as a brother or sister and wish them peace three times, then let them go and come back to yourself.

21

Rivero Sambation, a slightly flabby but congenial young man with a head of tight curls, not to mention a snappy dresser with an expensive penchant for those Richard James-style suits that accentuate your good bits and hide the bad, had always had unusual yearnings for what went on behind the scenes of everyday life and had never wanted to be a professional taxidermist. Sure it was fun as a hobby, but as a living it drained your soul. But when his father died and left him the family taxidermy business, he took the easy option and found himself trapped in a dead-end career, where his only relief came from attending so-called spirituality classes given by Lango Faldo, the world-famous spiritual teacher.

One day Lango, who was naturally possessed of strong intuition, took him aside and said, 'Sambation, I see a great future for you as a tarot card reader, a great future,' and passed him a worn, crumpled deck.

Closing down the family business immediately, Sambation set up shop in Brighton and was soon doing a brisk trade, even numbering royalty and foreign diplomats among his clientele. Indeed, it was said the wife of the world's biggest arms dealer never made a move without first consulting him by phone (for no less than €300 an hour! Not that he was euro-obsessed …)

But when Harvard Arequipa, slick-looking silver-haired lawyer for the estate of the late Rits Històrico, notorious underworld figure killed along with his minder, Capstan, by a simple flying kick to the temple delivered by Nervo Nergal, daring, dashing Brazilian Capoeira champion, walked in one morning to seek his psychic assistance in tracking down six million missing Swiss francs left in an expensive Italian attaché case under a parked car in New Mexico, and offering him twenty per cent if he retrieved the money, Rivero experienced a queer sense of foreboding.

In the cards he saw an attractive but obsessive woman, who worked in the arts, travelling to a desert island off the coast of West Africa. (He was that good.)

'There must be dozens of islands like that. Which one is it?' Arequipa stuck his face threateningly close to Sambation's. 'I don't know!' whimpered Rivero. Harvard grew impatient and slapped Sambation's face twice so forcefully his head hit the wall and he slumped to the floor unconscious. Through a hazy mist he saw a being (maybe an angel, maybe a barefoot doctor), who said, 'Be empty, trust your intuition and the answer will come,' then placed a soothing hand on the back of his head, tapped him lightly on the centre of the forehead three times and disappeared. Sambation came to, muttering, 'Gomera. She's on her way to Gomera.'

Harvard Arequipa smoothed back his silver hair, carefully placed a letter confirming the twenty per cent on the desk, slapped Sambation once more for good measure, then took the train to Gatwick and was on the first scheduled flight (he never flew chartered) out to Tenerife to catch a speedboat to Gomera the very next day.

If you're in a predicament and you can't see which way to go, repeat: 'I trust my intuition,' until you mean it. Then empty your mind of all thoughts by focussing on your breathing, gaze into the dark space between and behind your eyes, and ask your intuition to reveal the answer you need. Then forget all about it and in the hours or days that follow, the information will come in a dream, on the side of a passing van, in the snatch of a song or at the oddest moment.

22

As soon as Salbinellas Marina – one-time opportunist, ex-con woman, sometime girlfriend of notorious underworld figure the late Rits Historìco, now turned real estate broker selling pricey loft conversions in and around SoHo from her cellphone – met Porphyry Trents – one-time bigwig in Scottish Politics, ex-trapeze artist and Hollywood circus film star, now senator for New York – to show her round a loft on Mercer, she knew she would never want a man again. The electricity that passed between them was so startling, in fact, they both knew they'd be lovers for life.

But when Salbinellas moved in she had no idea Trents had a drink problem. When questioned, Trents broke down. 'It's the guilt. I can't live with it,' she explained between sobs.

'Guilt for what?' Salbinellas coaxed.

'Remember the retro-rock band, HT Russell?'

'You mean those guys who played a gig on a

platform suspended from two downtown sky-scrapers whose exact location was kept secret for obvious reasons, and who all got killed when the ropes snapped in a freak storm off the Atlantic?' asked Marina.

Porphyry nodded, 'Well it was me who gave them permission,' she said, and ran into the bath-room, where she threw up violently. Splashing cold water on her face, she glanced in the mirror and saw a being (maybe an angel, maybe a bare-foot doctor, maybe she was just drunk), who said, 'Guilt is just disguised fear of divine retribution of which you need have no fear. Each of us is respon-sible for our own realities. HT Russell knew the risks. Their death was their responsibility not yours. Stop destroying yourself, it won't help HT Russell or anyone else.' He then touched her lightly in the centre of her chest and was gone.

When Porphyry Trents walked out of the bath-room, she was a transformed woman. 'Come on,' she said to Salbinellas, throwing a few things in a suitcase, 'let's quit this crazy town. There's a power yoga retreat I was reading about on the semi-arid desert island of Gomera where Placentia Ordanato teaches. Let's go!'

If you're destroying yourself on account of some mis-conceived guilt, repeat the following affirmation till you mean it: 'By destroying myself, I am merely adding to the darkness of the world. By forgiving myself and creating myself anew, I add to the light. By increasing the light, I make up for any wrong I've done.'

23

After Salbinellas Marina – opportunist and one-time con woman, now New York real estate broker – left Nervo Nergal – daring, dashing Brazilian Capoeira champion – lying low in Bahia after he'd killed her boyfriend, Rits Historìco, notorious underworld figure along with his minder, Capstan, he (Nervo) went slowly mad.

One particularly sultry, brain-frying afternoon, flipping through a German magazine in the waiting room of a Freudian analyst he'd started seeing, he chanced upon an ad for a power yoga retreat on the semi-arid desert island of Gomera taught by Placentia Ordanato, the ravishing beauty who used to hold all of New York and London in the palm of her hand. Without waiting for his session or even thinking to offer to pay the cancellation fee, he ran home to his beach cabana, threw some things in an ordinary-looking bag and caught the first plane out via New York on a knock-down premium economy ticket. Sitting behind two women in business, whose faces he couldn't see, he was disturbed all night by an unusual variety of smooching noises they kept making as well as intermittent violent stomach cramps from a gastric flu he'd picked up at the airport cafeteria in Rio.

On his ninth trip to the toilet he went dizzy and collapsed momentarily over the sink, where in his delirious state, a being (maybe an angel, maybe a barefoot doctor) appeared up out of the plug hole and asked, 'What's up, Nervo?'

'I keep falling short. I lost control and killed two men with my own bare feet. I lost perspective over my childhood sweetheart who just left me a second time, I lost control of my mind and now I've lost control of my bowels. I've let myself down, I've let my family down, I've let my teachers down and I feel ashamed.'

'Aw, forget it kid. Firstly, no one, however well-trained or disciplined, is above human weakness. Secondly, though it's no vindication for murder, Rits had it coming to him. He was a notorious underworld figure. And the broad was up to no good anyway. And as for your guts, as soon as you accept yourself, they'll quieten down.' At which he touched Nervo's belly lightly and disappeared back down the plug hole.

Nervo came to from his delirium feeling unusually integrated, returned to his seat and newly oblivious to the squelchy, cooing noises emanating from the seats in front, fell fast asleep.

If you think you fall short of the ideal, repeat this affirmation in front of a mirror until you mean it: 'However much of an evil, no-good, low-down, worthless bum (I think) I've been, I am willing to accept myself fully for it, for only from that place can I go forward and make amends.'

✦

24

It took some minutes for Sister Kimbal Neosho, Buddhist nun – once Professo Expressional, one-time loving-relationships trainer, ex-preacher who'd undergone a sex-change – to get up off the floor where she lay panting with unrequited desire for Lango Faldo, world-famous spiritual teacher who had just refused her advances, and hurriedly left the Buddhist retreat she was running.

Pulling herself together, she sat down to meditate and, closing her eyes, saw a being (maybe an angel, maybe a barefoot doctor), who said, 'Hey, baby, it's not him you desire, it's the quality he represents.'

'You mean his breezy non-attachment?' asked Neosho. But the being just tapped her on her right breast and was gone.

Without once turning back, Neosho suddenly ran helter-skelter down the mountain to the local bar and fell into a chance conversation with Drifto

Continental, an unshaven, wind-burnt local drunk and divorce lawyer. 'I no longer feel attached to being a nun,' she confessed as she poured out her heart to this stranger.

'Well,' he said, eyeing her up briefly and finding her unremarkable yet somehow intriguing, 'It just so happens I've been scouring the internet and found this power yoga retreat on the semi-arid desert island of Gomera where Placentia Ordanata, who used to hold all New York and London in the palm of her hand, teaches. Fancy a trip?'

'What the hell, why not? But I'll need to stop by a store first to pick up some civvies,' Neosho replied nonchalantly.

She hurried in to the mall while he waited in his pick-up, and quickly forgetting her vows of asceticism, loaded a holdall with brightly coloured power yoga costumes, a little black number on the off chance she was invited anywhere smart, along with some basic cosmetics, skin products and après-sun, and quickly jumped in the pick-up just in time for Drifto to get them to San Francisco to board the flight to Tenerife via Madrid and catch the boat over to Gomera.

If your plans don't work out, use this as an opportunity to reconnect with the source of all being. Stand with your feet together and your arms outstretched to the sides so you form a cross. Visualize a vertical stream of light running from the sky down your spine to the centre of the Earth and a horizontal one going from left to right through your arms. Now reverse the visualization so the vertical stream goes up and the horizontal goes right to left. Then say: 'When my plans go wrong it's because something far better awaits me.' That's it.

25

Daveyroll Dùsh, Newcastle-born solar architect and trance DJ, had had enough watching the hippies doing t'ai chi in the sunset on the beach in Goa. He went back to his house with his retro flares flapping, and out of sheer boredom he stupidly swallowed three micro-dots of lysurgic acid, unaware they were treble strength. Before he could realize what was going on he had lost control of his mind.

As dimension gave way unto dimension and his ego began to disintegrate fully, a being materialized as if from the very atoms of the universe (maybe an angel, maybe a barefoot doctor) who said, 'Listen, Daveyroll, I'm not going to feed you any enlightening revelations – just get down to the semi-arid desert island of Gomera and do a power yoga retreat.'

'Who's teaching it?' asked Dùsh noncommittally.

'Placentia Ordanato,' replied the being patiently.

'Oh, the chick who used to hold the whole of New York and London in the palm of her hand. I'm there like a bear,' he struggled to reply, and without waiting politely to see whether the being had disappeared or not, stumbled rudely about throwing things in a technologically-advanced suitcase with wheels, swallowed a couple of Valium to settle his stomach and made straight for the airport, flying off via Mumbai and Addis Ababa without a second thought.

If an impulse grabs you with so much force you can't resist and see no real reason why you should, go with it for all it's worth, repeating the following affirmation as you go till you believe it: 'My life is nothing if it's not a rip-roaring adventure for everyone to enjoy.' That's better.

26

Placentia Ordanato, the ravishing beauty and power yoga instructor who once held all New York and London in the palm of her hand, walked into the makeshift office at the power yoga retreat she'd set up with Brandell Willard – one-time suicidal depressive, ex-drugs mule and con man turned mass-market producer and distributor of rubber and fetish wear – on a mountainside finca on the semi-arid desert island of Gomera, just as Brandell, beginning to feel the strain, put the phone down. Muttering half to himself without even looking up he mused incredulously: 'Looks like we've got a full fortnight next week, the bookings have been coming in thick and fast. It's amazing. I don't know what's going on.'

'Well, that's what we came here for, isn't it? I feel so at one with the creative force of all existence, I guess I must be manifesting well,' she replied, borderline goody-miss-two-shoes smugly.

Brandell hated her self-centred New Ageist approach and without warning flew into a sudden rage, accidentally – though Freud may have claimed intentionally – knocking her back with such force as he stormed past her through the open door that she jarred her neck, momentarily lost her studied composure and screamed: 'Now you've done it. My neck's gone out and I won't be able to teach the retreat!'

'Guess you must be manifesting well, then,' he mimicked, masking his own feelings of defeat, and walked outside to smoke a reefer.

As she struggled to regain her composure, Placentia felt a presence behind her and turning to look saw a being (maybe an angel, maybe a barefoot doctor), doing an easy salute to the sun, who turned and with a focused beam of energy, said, 'Maybe you have been being a bit self-centred and stiff-necked about things, Placentia. Ease off and everything will fall into place!' Then doing a double back-flip, disappeared through a wall.

Feeling suddenly capable of anything, she grabbed herself by the temples and jerking her head to the side, cricked her neck back into place.

'I guess I was a bit of an arsehole back there,' she said by way of apology as she approached

Brandell, 'I was masking my feelings of inadequacy behind a layer of control.'

'Oh, for heaven's sake,' spat Brandell, his eyes rolling upwards to mask his inability to be vulnerable and, wishing to avoid a sentimental reconciliation, spun on his heel and walked away.

If people are accusing you of being too self-centred and smug, maybe they're right. Stop and consider the miracle of your existence and how improbable it all is, then repeat this affirmation till you feel a subtle shift in consciousness: 'With every breath I take, I realize I know less and less, I grow more and more aware of the improbability of existence and feel more and more gratitude. It's incredible to be here with everyone!'

27

Bambassi Rongalon had always had misgivings about becoming a rent boy, not just because it went against his faith, but also because he was fundamentally heterosexual and the sex made him uncomfortable. Limping stiffly home after a particularly heavy job, his shaven, tattooed head aching, he decided to give it all up, to turn away from the big bucks and become a postman or a newsreader on local radio, both jobs he'd always fancied.

What he hadn't reckoned on was Dwight Xorblyn, a secret service agent who'd been trailing him for weeks who had been particularly interested to observe him through a two-way mirror on his knees, in a compromising position with a leading Chinese Politburo mover and shaker.

Made the scapegoat in what turned out to be the biggest blazing spy scandal in decades, Bambassi was sent down for eighteen years on trumped-up charges. As he gazed wistfully at the glaring naked bulb in the ceiling during his first night of captivity, after being severely gang-raped by a group of depraved inmates and a couple of warders, he perceived a being (maybe an angel, maybe a barefoot doctor, maybe just a trick of the light), who said, 'You feel bad now, Rongalon, but deliverance is at hand – forgive me for this ...' and then proceeded to kick him hard in the shin.

Bambassi's knee jerked reflexively, his foot kicked the slop bucket, the slop shot up (improbably) and hit the naked light bulb, causing an unlikely short circuit which took out all the lighting and unlocked all the security doors. In the ensuing confusion, Rongalon made his escape. Stopping just long enough to pick up a Bavarian-style trilby to cover his tattoos and a false passport from an Albanian connection in North London, he managed to make it down to Luton airport where he took the first flight out, which happened to be going to Tenerife. On arrival he noticed a flyer someone had dropped by the taxi rank advertising a local power yoga retreat, and took the first ferry over to the semi-arid desert island of Gomera.

Be alert and perceptive to the slightest shift in the action. Always be ready for an exciting change in your circumstances. To release inertia, exhale. Inhale deeply to draw in new impetus to move on with your life story, then repeat this till you feel it in your bones: 'Nothing is fixed. Everything is possible. I now move forward into a new phase of unprecedented adventure.' (That's it.)

28

Nothing happened in this fable. It was late. No one was in town. No beings, (whether angels or barefoot doctors) appeared. Nothing changed. (For once).

If nothing appears to be happening for you right now, it may seem dull, but, baby, don't feel too sorry for yourself. There are plenty of beings (maybe angels, maybe barefoot doctors) who would love to do nothing for the length of an entire fable. Yes, boredom is a scourge but start breathing freely and centering yourself and you'll soon notice how exciting it is simply to be alive. Say: 'I now take full advantage of all available downtime and allow myself humbly to enjoy the visceral sensation of being here!'

29

As an antidote to her stressful life as a prima ballerina, Dunkalini Unga, the superbly toned, bright-eyed former Capoeira student of daring, dashing Brazilian champion Nervo Nergal, took up thatching as a hobby and became so skilled that her fame quickly spread and she began to receive commissions from far and wide. One day, she received a request from a multimillionaire in Dubai to thatch the roof of his twenty-three-story office block for a fabulous tax-free sum far exceeding her annual ballet salary and benefits package. She jacked in the job without a moment's hesitation and flew straight there, setting to work immediately before giving herself any time to acclimatize.

Not appreciating the sun's strength, she'd thatched nearly a third of the roof when she succumbed to sunstroke, lost her footing and tumbled in a clumsy facsimile of a Capoeira cartwheel headfirst over the edge.

Just as her crown was about to hit the ground, a being appeared, (maybe an angel, maybe a barefoot doctor), who miraculously broke her fall by catching her deftly by the ankles and holding her suspended one inch above the ground so that she could see up his nose. 'Hey baby,' the being said, 'this presages a big change in your life, I can see it intuitively.'

'It does?' Dunkalini Unga asked, bewildered. But the being had disappeared, thoughtlessly leaving her head to drop with a muffled thud onto the hot dusty pavement.

Righting herself painfully and wiping a stray strand of thatch from her eye, she noticed a flyer on the pavement advertising a power yoga retreat on the semi-arid desert island of Gomera. The words resonated somewhere deep inside her and as soon as she'd finished off the roof and collected the cash she made straight for the airport, without even bothering with duty-free, and took the first flight to Madrid, from where she caught a connecting flight to Tenerife and a ferry over to Gomera.

Never fear the dramatic twists and turns of life, for it is these that trigger the necessary and inevitable change required for you to grow to full potential in this life. Reality conforms to the beliefs you hold about it. That's the basis of magic. Hence all change is good if you believe it is. To encourage this belief start method acting it by repeating till you mean it: 'All change is good.' Good.

30

Bleckstrak Nengervan, successful Norwegian club promoter and recruitment consultant, was feeling spiritually blocked. His new muted yellow Porsche 911-4, Italian designer minimalist trainers and central Manchester warehouse apartment were no longer cutting the existential mustard. After a particularly lucrative night that left him quite nonplussed, something deep inside snapped and, much to the consternation of his fiancée, friends and colleagues, he flew to Bangkok and enrolled at the Wat Po temple on a three-week intensive course of Thai massage. There he met a German explorer on his way to the Andaman Sea to hang out with the Bugis pirates and, without even waiting to finish the massage course, set off with the German and wound up washing dishes on a pirate ship.

One night, after thieving a cargo of wool from a New Zealand-registered freighter, the pirate ship was caught in an unseasonal squall, ran aground on rocks and capsized.

As Nengervan lay floating semi-conscious on a piece of driftwood with rain and spray splashing his face, a being appeared in a raindrop, maybe an angel, maybe a barefoot doctor. 'You had a good thing going, Nengervan. Perhaps there was no need to react so extremely to your spiritual ennui. It was just a sign that something great was about to happen. You could have stayed in Manchester if you wanted rain on your face. The antidote to ennui is to be found inside,' he said, gesturing at Nengervan's heart. Then he disappeared back into the void.

Nengervan came to with a start, just as a giant wave was about to engulf him. Drawing on his innermost reserves and the years he'd spent as a youth skate-boarding the streets of Oslo, he stood up on the driftwood board and rode the wave back to shore. From there he stopped in Pukhet just long enough to pick up a change of clothes before heading off to Bangkok where he bought a ticket on the first flight to Manchester.

Standing at the check-in desk, he glanced down at his shoes as he'd always done since childhood to reassure himself he was actually there, and his attention was diverted by a flyer for a power yoga retreat on the semi-arid desert island of Gomera that someone had dropped on the floor.

Something about it struck a mellifluous chord inside him, prompting him to pay a $76 supplement to take the first flight to Madrid instead, from there to catch a connection to Tenerife and the boat over to Gomera.

When spiritual ennui is threatening your peace of mind, resist the temptation to overreact. Breakthrough will come as soon as you become still and accept where you are right now. Breathe in silently, without effort, to the count of eight, and then out to the count of nine. Repeat this cycle seven times, affirming: 'Everything worthwhile arises out of stillness.'

31

Walking down the Champs Elysées, puffed with pride after doing a turn at a bar currently favoured by the fashionable Parisian set, Swink Taloon, an up-and-coming experimental breaks DJ fresh out of Southend-on-Sea with a cocky rude-boy short-step swagger, exuded a distinct air of insouciant arrogance quite incongruous with his grand and elegant surroundings.

But under the insouciance was anxiety. His lawyer, silver-haired Harvard Arequipa, was in the middle of crucial negotiations with a well-financed independent dance label for Taloon's next mix album, but had failed to phone him as promised.

Pulling his voice-activated phone from his pocket, Taloon placed a call to Arequipa's office only to be informed that he'd gone on urgent business to a power yoga retreat on the semi-arid desert island of Gomera. So great was his need for the record company advance and figuring mistakenly that it wouldn't be hard to track Arequipa down in a one-horse place like that, Taloon took a cab to Charles de Gaulle to catch the first flight to Barcelona to pick up a connecting flight to Tenerife and catch the ferry over to Gomera.

Flying over the Pyrenees, the weather was turbulent, the plane lurched violently and lost altitude with such force that he was sure his number was up. But as his life flashed in clichéd style before his eyes, a being, (maybe an angel, maybe a barefoot doctor), appeared out of the seat pocket in front of him and said, 'Relax, Swink, it's not your time yet. And it's not just so you can pick up the cheque for your advance ...'

'How d'you know I was thinking about that?'

'I can read your mind. The reason you're not going to die yet is because you've got a musical mission to accomplish. Anyway, there's no need to overreact to a bit of turbulence. Planes are built to take it.' At which the being disappeared back into the seat pocket, the plane gained altitude, and a few minutes later made a steady descent and successful landing at Barcelona, with Swink repeating, 'Hardcore,' over and over in his head like a mantra.

Don't be ashamed if you appear to be motivated by nothing more meaningful than a fast buck. Beneath your surface desires you are on a mission of great significance to the world. Before sleeping, ask your unconscious mind to reveal it to you in your dreams.

32

Lango Faldo, one-time world-famous spiritual teacher, ex-personal fitness trainer and mainstream family entertainment TV presenter, recently dropped for losing ratings among the youth audience, especially the lucrative under-threes, felt as low as a discarded sweet wrapper stuck in a fox-hole as he ambled aimlessly along Sunset Boulevard.

Stepping carelessly off the curb, he didn't notice the speeding mid-range sports utility vehicle until its bumper caught him rudely in the thighs and hurled him a clear nineteen feet in the air. Landing heavily on a passing doomsday preacher, breaking the preacher's collarbone in three places in the process, Lango lost consciousness.

From the depths of the void, a being, (maybe an angel, maybe a barefoot doctor), pirouetting in what looked like a rose-coloured tutu, called out, 'Lango, don't doubt yourself for a moment. Just because things look bleak is no reason to believe they actually are. Is there any reason to think the adventure's going to stop now?' At which the being slapped him briskly on the left cheek, spun on his toes and disappeared back into the void.

When Lango came to, he extricated himself from the grip of the preacher, who, though in severe pain, was attempting to warn him to relinquish Babylon before it was all too late, walked off down the street and stumbled blindly through the first open doorway he found, hoping he could find somewhere to wash his face and freshen up.

The timeshare broker's receptionist assumed he was the new salesman and thrust some airline tickets in his hand, sending him off on the first plane to Madrid to pick up the connection to Tenerife to start work the following day, hustling tourists on the street to invest in timeshare apartments, chalet-style bungalows with a shared pool or private villas.

If you fear life's beneficence has forsaken you, relax and give yourself up to the mystery of the adventure. Drop the story you're carrying around about yourself and become empty and humble for a while. Before you've had time to say 'Snopme Chaddelow', life will shower you with a thousand and eight unexpected blessings. Be grateful for this rare opportunity to witness all life's remarkable spectacles around you and simply ask out loud, over and over, 'Whatever next?'

33

Old school friend of daring, dashing, Brazilian Capoeira champion Nervo Nergal, Snopme Chaddelow sported a conservative, dressed-down banker look of polo shirts, khaki chinos and boat shoes, along with a mischievous twinkle in his eye. He'd always found it hard to explain how he'd ended up heading the largest private security firm in Argentina, and how it had led circuitously to him getting busted for financing the biggest ever importation of acid for the fast-growing, almost world-class Buenos Aires club scene. Now sitting between two burly cops in the back of a speeding police car, heading downtown to bribe the chief of police, he decided enough was enough. Having bought his release in US dollars, cleared his desk at the office, and thrown a few things hastily into a brand-name sports bag, he jumped on a plane to Rio De Janeiro to visit Nervo, the only person who'd understand his plight. Unfortunately by the time he'd trekked all the way to Bahia he found that Nervo had gone to some lousy power yoga retreat on the semi-arid desert island of Gomera, run by Placentia Ordanato, ravishing beauty who used to hold all of New York and London in the palm of her hand, without so much as letting him know.

Wandering about dazed and not knowing where to go next in his life, he stumbled into the hinterlands and was only mildly nonplussed to run into an elderly Welsh hippie studying shaman-ism with the local tribe, who gave him a pipe of mind-altering dimethyltriptamine, more com-monly known as DMT or 'businessman's lunch', to smoke.

As dimension disintegrated into dimension, instead of the little green men the Welshman had warned him of, appeared a being, (maybe an angel, maybe a barefoot doctor), who said simply, 'Follow the instincts in your guts, Chaddelow,' then realiz-ing only shock tactics would work on someone with the kind of defences indicated by Chaddelow's lousy dress sense, reluctantly punched him moder-ately hard in the solar plexus and disappeared just as the drug's effects were wearing off.

Chaddelow came to feeling like he'd been reluctantly punched moderately hard in the gut.

'I've got to get out of here,' he said aloud to himself, 'I need to go home to Brighton.'

Wandering down the Lanes behind the Pavilion now, he found it hard to explain how he'd got there or why he'd wandered into the shopfront premises of Rivero Sambation, snappily-dressed psychic and tarot card reader.

'If I'm not mistaken, I see you settling down here in a small apartment on the front and buying a timeshare in Tenerife for vacations,' Sambation said slowly, looking up from the cards. His words rang a bell somewhere deep inside Chaddelow's head, and, wasting no time, he was on the first charter flight from Gatwick to Tenerife the very next day.

If you find yourself in a quandary, let your mind be still and listen for the promptings from your guts. Say about eighteen times: 'My instincts always lead me right.'

INTERMISSION

(And quick word of advice from a being, maybe an angel, maybe a barefoot doctor, whom you could easily imagine poking his head in a cheeky fashion out through the crimson velvet curtains in the interval, just when you'd got back into your seat and were preparing to eat your tub of ice-cream or what-have-you):

As a being, my orbit takes me to many far-flung places and affords me the opportunity of being privy to many characters and their most intimate stories from the inside out, as it were. What I've noticed, as I'm sure you've noticed yourself, is that a chain of events involving many characters and thus lending the illusion of a story, necessarily involves many apparent twists and turns and these can sometimes make your head spin if you are trying to remain abreast of the action. It's as if you're attempting to play the part of the all-seeing, all-knowing consciousness of the universe itself, whilst also having to conduct a responsible life and maintain some semblance of order in your mind, which as you're probably already finding out, is no mean feat – hence the warning at the beginning of the book that this will either heal you or make you go insane.

To promulgate the former rather than the latter, it is strongly advised you take a short break before reading any further. This is precisely what all the characters hitherto mentioned have done. In fact they are all, strangely and coincidentally, at this precise moment enjoying a quiet siesta. Brandell Willard, Lango Faldo, Dallalia Wilkins, Salbinellas Marina, Porphyry Trents, Nervo Nergal, Rivero Sambation, Harvard Arequipa, Swink Taloon, Sister Kimbal Neosho, Snopme Chaddelow, Daveyroll Dùsh, Bambassi Rongalon, Dunkalini Unga, Bleckstrak Nengervan, Placentia Ordanato and even the late Rits Historìco, his late minder Capstan and the late retro rock band, HT Russell – the whole motley crew – are all fast asleep.

You may wish, without waking them, to quietly revisit their stories before moving on. On the other hand, all vacuums are soon filled and while they sleep the world continues to spin with new, unfamiliar characters who've been waiting in the wings biding their time playing out their various life-stories, and who are now ready to step onto the stage of your imagination if you are ready for them.

So if you've finished your ice-cream and done whatever it is you've had to, you're sufficiently familiar with all the above characters not to fall prey to confusion with the introduction of more, you're entirely sure your intention is to be healed rather than to go insane – not that there isn't a fine line between the two – and you're sitting, lying or standing quite comfortably, the story can go on ...

34

Thick of thigh and keen of eye, Midlands-born Kwipstah Tonk, youth marketing consultant, had worked his way up from tea boy to managing director at leading east London marketing and PR house, Biscuit, in only three years and knew a thing or two about the back-stabbing that went on in boardrooms. Still flying perilously high on the post-boom era of youth marketing and a few lucky breaks, he reeled out his well-rehearsed though fundamentally insubstantial recipe for success to everyone gathered round the boardroom table to hear his pitch at one of the world's most prominent multi-national arms manufacturers.

'Global identity, it's all down to identity – branding, in other words – and of course building global brand loyalty. If you want your product to dominate the youth market when you finally roll it out, and then radiate outwards to the other consumer sectors with a steady trickle-down effect, you need a concerted guerrilla marketing campaign that encourages the customer to feel she's discovered the brand for herself. You need to carry the brand promise through to the end user by promoting club nights around the world, paying special attention to the fast up-and-coming world-class, recession-proof Buenos Aires market, release mix albums, do live webcasts, publish an online and hard-copy monthly magazine, produce clothing and general related lifestyle products and stage miscellaneous promotional events,' Tonk explained, his gold bracelet clanking into his gold and titanium watch as he banged the table to emphasize 'miscellaneous'.

'You got it,' stumped up the chairman with a hint of a Sicilian-American accent, after chewing contemplatively on the end of his cigar, ruminating on what Tonk had said. He knew the kid was full of shit but liked his style and the way he strung the jargon together. 'Collect your money on the way out,' he said.

Whooping and hollering along the street, mentally calculating how to spend his windfall, Tonk was unaware that he had walked into the middle of a turf war in full throttle taking place between rival drug gangs of Turks and Albanians, until a stray bullet caught him squarely in the left shoulder.

Lying on the operating table pumped full of anaesthetic, a being appeared in inner space, (maybe an angel, maybe a barefoot doctor), who, holding open his ear, not brusquely but firmly to ensure he was heard, enquired, 'Tonk, you familiar with the concept of karma – cause and effect – as you sow, so shall you reap? Because what just happened was your karma for getting into bed with destructive elements for the sake of a quick buck, not to mention for talking a load of marketing baloney so shamelessly. It's not to do with punishment, simply to do with corrective signals being sent your way.' He then released Tonk's ear and promptly disappeared.

By the time his new prosthetic arm, adorned with gold bracelet and gold and titanium watch, was fully functional, Tonk had already resigned from his marketing post and taken a part-time job in a global activism organization as events coordinator. His first brief was an ETA fundraiser stunt, comprising scaling the walls of the local TV station on Tenerife and hanging an 'ETA is better!' banner, for which he was promptly arrested and thrown in a holding cell.

If you're feeling dubious about the way you've been conducting yourself lately, check what's motivating you. If it's merely self-interest, look for ways of contributing something worthwhile to balance the karmic scales. Affirm this: 'I give the gift of myself with every breath I exhale.' Hold your awareness of bringing the gift of your being to everyone's benefit and before you can say Laborimu Spinnij your life will have taken on an entirely new meaning.

35

Laborimu Spinnij, fading star of critically lauded foreign arthouse movies, turned slowly on her Pilates
exercise mat, the taut muscles of her still fine pair of
legs flexing, as the door to her four-bedroom, con-
ventionally-styled holiday home in Marbella
opened suddenly. Her late husband, Dazlo Spinnij,
retired GM food scientist, philanthropist and weekend acrobat for fun and self-expression, had only
been bumped off the week before, shot stone dead
for failing to pay an old gambling debt, by a hit
man working for a group of local ex-pat English
gangland members. Her nerves were on edge in
case anything should go wrong with the will. She
needed the money to finance a movie to be directed
by her longstanding teenage lover that would
one day gross, she hoped, more than any other
movie ever and in which she was to make her star
comeback and attain her well-deserved screen
immortality.

Standing framed in the doorway, backlit by the glare of a distant floodlight creating a halo effect, was a being, (maybe an angel, maybe a barefoot doctor, she couldn't tell – there was only a silhouette), who said, 'Laborimu, the immortality you seek on celluloid or digital formats is illusory. It will go the way of all form and end in a slow dissolve. To live forever, you must identify solely with that within which never dies because it is never born.'

Before Laborimu had time to ask, 'What the deuce...?' the being had disappeared as if someone had cut the film. Filling the space where he'd stood was a delivery truck with 'Power Yoga Tools For The Professional' emblazoned on its side. Something struck a resonant chord inside her. Searching first for 'tools' and then for 'power yoga', her rusty old laptop turned up a retreat on the relatively nearby semi-arid desert island of Gomera, run by Placentia Ordanata, who, if she wasn't mistaken, used to hold all of New York and London in the palm of her hand.

Leaving a hurried note to her teenage boyfriend, Laborimu threw some things in an expensive, slightly out-of-date designer travelling bag, and took the first plane going south out of Malaga.

If you're worried about leaving your immortal mark on the world, stop. Inside you, deep in the core of your being, is the you who watches, lifetime after lifetime, as the local drama unfolds. This is your immortal spirit. Every time you breathe in, imagine you can see and feel the presence of your own immortal spirit filling and surrounding you as a large luminescent being, and every time you breathe out, imagine you are that being. In any case, that spark is who you are and it's just a matter of time before you know it too – if you don't already. So for immortality, it's spark, not mark, from now on!

36

Standing on the veranda of her expensively refurbished mountainside finca, bought as a winter weekend retreat to indulge her extreme sado-masochistic proclivities in relative seclusion, Quimper Frondondo, severely dressed multi-millionaire heiress of one of the most noble families in all Madrid, who having received an English public school education went on to gain minor fame as a national TV newsreader in the UK, with a strong 18 to 25-year-old, predominantly ABC male following, who found her severe look and neatly tied-back hair unsettlingly beguiling, was starting to wonder who all the unusual-looking people were who kept rolling up in dribs and drabs at the next finca down the mountainside, above the bay on the semi-arid desert island of Gomera.

Having made sure the dungeon in the cellar was clean, all the torture instruments were in working order and the rack oiled just in case she should get lucky later, curiosity got the better of her, so she slipped into a casual but elegant twin-set with colour-contrasted low-heeled sling-back shoes and walked down the mountain to explore.

Slowing down briefly as she always did to admire the view, her heel got caught on a branch and she went tumbling over the rocks, twisting both ankles, dislocating an arm and sustaining a mild concussion. Managing to pull a phone from her clutch bag, she called for an air ambulance and settled herself down to await its arrival. Entering a state of mild delirium from the pain, which had now become excruciating, she could have sworn she was dancing the foxtrot with a being (maybe an angel, maybe a barefoot doctor), who, as he guided her dexterously round the astral dance-floor, asked, 'What are you so ashamed of, Frondondo?'

'What makes you assume I'm ashamed of any-thing?' she asked, mildly indignant, with a hint of Iberian hauteur.

'I don't assume anything, I see it. All that equipment in your dungeon? You are suffering from innate shame and, unwilling to face it, project it out instead onto your victims,' replied the being.

'But I know what I'm doing and I never cause any lasting damage or scars ...' her voice trailed off as his words found resonance within.

Noticing the subtle shift of energy as she momentarily released her preconceptions, the being suddenly straightened and said, 'Hold tight, baby, your life's about to go through such a change you won't know what's hit you,' at which he span his whole body into a blur and exploded into a thousand stars.

When she emerged, neatly bandaged, from the unusually technologically well-equipped Tenerife hospital A and E, Frondondo was a fetching sight and one which did not go unnoticed by Snopme Chaddelow, ex-head of the largest private security firm in Argentina, recently busted for financing a huge consignment of acid, now resident in Brighton but looking to buy a Tenerife timeshare, who strode up to her without hesitation and asked her out on a date there and then.

If you suspect you harbour deep shame about your person and may be projecting it in punishing ways onto others, stop and turn your attention inwards. There, deep inside your solar plexus, where you process information as well as food, tell yourself confidently: 'What I am is pure and beautiful!' Repeat this daily and your whole way of interacting with others will be transformed for the better. By the same token, or maybe by a different token altogether, if you've been hesitating from asking someone out on a date or something similar, for fear of catching them at an inopportune moment, hesitate so no longer. Be bold, take a risk and ask them now – if only for the theatre of it.

✦

37

Aspiring novelist Zank Drazdan III never could figure out how he'd ever got mixed up in being a CIA field-operative spying on London. Maybe it was revenge on his father, Zank Drazdan Junior, as his analyst had suggested, for being such a counter-culturalist and losing old Zank Drazdan Senior's money. Maybe it was just the desire for a cheap thrill. But as he looked out now from his penthouse lair high above the Thames, he was beginning to wonder if he wasn't in over his head.

Suddenly, he was overcome by a nauseating wave of panic at the sound of the entry phone buzzing. Stopping in front of a mirror to ask himself what to do, instead of the expected reflection of his own familiar, mildly Central European features, the face of a being, (maybe an angel, maybe a barefoot doctor), stared back at him and said, 'Don't panic, stay cool buddy, it's all gonna work out fine. It has to, we've got a project for you.'

'More spying?' asked Drazdan, betraying a hint of paranoia.

'No, Zank, it's that novel you've got inside you somewhere.'

As Zank turned away from the mirror the being vanished, but on the bed was a parcel.

Figuring rightly that there wasn't much time before the trapdoor on his personal liberty closed for good, he opened the parcel, read the instructions quickly and put on the enclosed false goatee, black leather beret, which he set at a jaunty angle, dark Italian suit, smartly ironed, fine cotton matching T-shirt, well-shined black leather shoes and discrete designer wrap-around shades, which he pulled down hard over his eyes. He threw a few things in a brand name duffle bag, made for the service elevator and set off just in the nick of time, via City Airport, Madrid and Tenerife for the relatively unspoiled semi-arid desert island of Gomera in the Canaries off the coast of North Africa, popular with hippie-types according to the instructions, where no one would ever think to look for him, to write his novel.

If you're waiting around for a being, supernatural or otherwise, to give you permission to get started on a creative project, wait no longer. Here's your permission: start now.

38

Pefflon Isissies, priest and occasional freelance journalist, had always been hung up about his name and had no regrets about changing it by deed-poll as soon as he had been defrocked and discretely discharged from the priesthood for various dubious indulgences, including sniffing copious quantities of ketamin, cocaine and a profusion of young girls' mountainbike seats.

Signing a credit card slip now as he checked out of an upmarket Amsterdam hotel under his new name, Chevrie Hamptu, made him smile. No longer would people take the piss. He was a new man, a free man. And as he wandered euphorically through the red-light district, he whistled a little tune of liberation.

But going from coffee shop to coffee shop, sampling every kind of cannabis available, was becoming tedious, so, stopping at a head shop he purchased a few grams of Hawaiian mushrooms, to which he added half a trip, a couple of pills of questionable composition and three valium to take the edge off. He guzzled the entire melange in one, chased by a stiff glass of scotch.

Seweppta Conchaxto, dark, curly-haired itinerant, half-gypsy, half-Colombian futures trader with an hourglass figure, was on her way to start a prestigious new job in Frankfurt. She watched with amusement as Chevrie wobbled purposefully along, occasionally bumping into people, once almost inadvertently stepping off into the canal.

Something about him intrigued her. It could have been his missing left foot, his over-developed biceps from using crutches, his crooked teeth or the deep dent on the side of his head from being beaten senseless once with a nine iron golf club. It could have been his piercing semi-vacant stare. She wasn't sure. But she knew at once that she wanted his babies.

Sticking out her foot as he ambled by, she caused him to trip and fall heavily, break his two front teeth and painfully stub his stump. She waited for him to struggle to his good foot and wipe the blood from his mouth on the sleeve of his hemp jacket before asking coyly, as an opening line, 'Excuse me, do I know you from somewhere?'

'No, why?' Chevrie asked, slightly taken aback as he struggled to stand upright. She said nothing but allowed her smile to caress his eyes briefly.

'Where are you heading?' he asked, recovering, noticing her passport laying casually on the table next to her cappuccino.

'Frankfurt, and you?' she asked, noticing the sunblock he was carrying.

'To cover a story for Reuters about Placentia Ordanato, the ravishing beauty who used to hold all of New York and London in the palm of her hand and who is setting up a power yoga retreat on the semi-arid desert island of Gomera. Fancy?'

Seweppta momentarily considered the million-plus annual salary with bonus and healthcare plan and Franz Bisch, the wealthy playboy waiting for her in his luxury townhouse in Frankfurt. She hesitated a moment. 'Why not?' she answered suddenly, casting a glance at his crooked, broken teeth.

Before setting off for the south, Chevrie treated Seweppta to a similar drug cocktail as the one he was beginning to come down from and had another himself. Within an hour they were both so mashed up they didn't even notice a being, (maybe an angel, maybe a barefoot doctor, maybe just a passing strawberry masquerading as a bare-foot doctor), trying to vehemently warn them of something, though no one ever discovered what.

Luckily, an utterly random, coincidental and totally unexpected neutron bomb, set off as a decoy by nuclear terrorist Glednel Jiltch, only damaged one runway and a few planes at Schippol Airport and they were able to take off for Tenerife after only nine hours delay.

Sometimes you don't need spiritual advice from angels or barefoot doctors. Sometimes you just need to get out of it, Dionyssian-style, and let things take care of themselves. Get dressed in your party clothes and indulge in forgetting yourself for an hour or two.

39

When Uttlu Rormatage found his wife in bed with her dental hygienist he sued for divorce, lost the house and all its contents, lost custody of his six children and was landed with a A$72,000 legal bill which wiped him clean out.

Now sitting hunched over in the dingy toilet of his small rented flat in downtown Sydney, he found it hard to see the point of carrying on. So demoralized was he that, after washing his hands and putting on an old sports jacket, he walked pensively to the nearby metro station, waited for the first train and was about to jump on the tracks, when a being (maybe an angel, maybe a barefoot doctor, maybe just his conscience), grabbed him from behind, pulled him back from the edge and said, 'Listen Uttlu, jumping now won't solve a thing. You'll come straight back as a possum or something worse, your six kids will hate your memory for the rest of their lives and when the police search your flat, they'll find all those women's clothes you've been dressing up in at weekends. On top of that, you'll freak the train driver out and he'll have to waste hours in post-traumatic stress counselling.'

'I'd rather that than having to face the future a ruined man,' Uttlu replied with a hopeless expression in his voice.

'There is no future, Uttlu, only the present exists. Take it moment by moment and you'll get through this in no time. Out of this darkness will come great light. Trust that. Give yourself a while to think about it and if you still want to die, then go ahead,' said the being empathetically, and then disappeared.

Uttlu stopped and thought about what the being had said. It made sense. But not everything has to make sense, he thought to himself, as the next train came roaring out of the tunnel and a random fair dodger running away from a platform guard brushed past him making him lose his balance just as he was about to step back from the edge, causing him instead to fall onto the tracks.

Sometimes, when you get too busy trying to make sense of things and it gives you a headache, ease off and let things happen of their own accord whether they seem to make sense or not. Affirm: 'I stop making sense now and allow life to happen as it will.'

40

On leaving casualty after twisting both ankles and dislocating an arm, minor celebrity Quimper Frondondo, severely dressed newsreader on mainstream British TV and member of one of the most noble families in all Madrid, was asked out on a date by Snopme Chaddelow, ex-head of the largest private security firm in Argentina, recently busted for drugs, now living back in his home town of Brighton, but currently out looking to buy a timeshare apartment or small villa on Tenerife. She accepted immediately. 'Where shall we go?' she asked.

'How about we go eat at a Chinese restaurant then maybe you could help me look for a timeshare apartment or small villa?' Snopme proposed eagerly.

'Well, my ankles are quite painful, but it sounds like fun. Let's do it.'

After dinner, they were accosted on the street

by Lango Faldo, one-time world-famous spiritual teacher, ex-personal fitness trainer and failed family entertainment TV presenter, now working as a timeshare salesman hustling tourists on the streets of Tenerife. He took them immediately to see a timeshare near the police station where Kwipstah Tonk, ex-youth marketing consultant turned activist, was being detained in a holding cell for scaling the wall of the TV station, at the precise moment that the ground shook from a 6.9 earthquake, demolishing the police station.

Struggling to free his leg from under a fallen RSJ, the pain became so intense that Tonk lost his nerve and was about to faint when a being, (maybe an angel, maybe a barefoot doctor), appeared out of the rubble, lifted the girder single-handedly, said, 'Run!' then disappeared in a cloud of dust.

Tonk wasted no time. Without bothering to tidy his bed he made a hasty escape and ran straight into Lango, Snopme and Quimper. The latter, clapping eyes on Tonk brushing dust awkwardly from his tousled hair with his prosthetic arm while clutching his freshly mangled leg, fell instantly, insanely in love.

Don't hang around waiting for some being to free you from your self-made prison. Affirm: 'By following the fascination in my heart, I am always delivered to where it's best for me.'

41

When Uttlu Rormatage, who, having found his wife in bed with her dental hygienist, lost all his money and custody of his six children in the divorce case, fell on the tracks in front of the oncoming Sydney metro train, he was sure his number was up. He was just about to pray for absolution when the metro-dedicated generator unexpectedly packed up, causing the live rail to go dead and the train to grind to a sudden halt three and a half centimetres from his right shoulder.

In his state of shocked confusion, not knowing whether to laugh or cry, a being appeared, (maybe an angel, maybe a barefoot doctor), who said, 'Your time on Earth is evidently not meant to be over yet, Uttlu. Get up off the rails before they sort out the generator, go home, shower, and search your soul to discover your true mission. Once you have found it, the trifling matter of losing your wife, your children and all your money will become a distant memory.'

In his state of shock, Uttlu didn't quite catch everything the being had said, but the being had disappeared before he had a chance to ask him to repeat it. By the time he got home, all he remembered was the bit about taking a shower, which he did, and as the water caressed his aching bones, his life's mission suddenly came to him in a flash.

Wasting no time at all, he enrolled in hairdressing school and as soon as his qualification came through he flew straight to Tenerife, where he'd heard there might be an opening for him to establish a low to mid-range beachfront salon.

Don't feel you have to let things get so bad you want to die before you start to live out your life's dream. Next time you're in the shower, ask your higher self to reveal the next step of your adventure to you, then take that step with boldness and aplomb.

42

Janko Poonanah, infamous West African doyen of Parisian haute couture, was suffering from a spiritual ennui that nothing could allay. Even though both his diffusion and exclusive couture clothing lines had taken the world by storm and his perfumes and accessories were on sale in every high street from Bangor to Addis Ababa; even though not a style magazine was printed anywhere in the world without a mention or photograph of him with his debonair looks and trademark blue fez somewhere within its glossy folds; and even though he could walk freely into the VIP rooms of the best clubs from Sheffield to Buenos Aires, he just couldn't shake the gnawing sense of discontentedness in his gut. He'd even tried spirituality, had actually studied with the once great Lango Faldo, but it had made him queasy.

Perhaps he'd been watching too many Hollywood movies, but sitting now in his Kreutzberg penthouse looking out over the drab

Berlin skyline, he couldn't escape the conclusion that perpetrating an act of mass destruction would be the only antidote to his existential angst.

Wasting no time, he trawled the internet for a couple of days until he found a site selling sarin nerve gas. Hesitantly he typed in his credit card details for a large enough quantity to wipe out an entire city, lit a Havana cigar, then sat back and ruminated a while before finally emailing the company who manufactured his perfume to warn them of a new, highly volatile secret compound which he wished to have added to bolster the base note of his top-selling fragrance line.

Walking out onto his balcony to check how he was feeling inside he was surprised by a being, (maybe an angel, maybe a barefoot doctor), climbing over the railing who said, 'Killing off your customers in this way may bring momentary distraction, but then you'll find yourself right back where you started. The only way to overcome your ennui is to go within on a daily basis. Don't fight the ennui. Discontent is part c⌐ the human condition. Accept that and everything will be fine.'

Poonanah thought carefully about what the being had said and then replied dismissively, 'Leave me alone, will you?' But the being had already disappeared over the edge.

Two days later, just as the sarin nerve gas was being added to the base notes of his best-selling fragrance line, a new designer suddenly became all the rage and the entire Poonanah brand was now officially considered yesterday's dinner. His enhanced fragrance was dumped on an obscure third world market, eventually killing nearly two-thirds of the adult population, an event which merited a small article on the back page of one or two newspapers and Poonanah, feeling mildly disheartened, moved to Tenerife and opened a beachfront bar called Janko's.

When existential ennui is causing you to think of doing harm to others, stop and remember that any harm you do will come back to you threefold. When beset by destructive urges, antidote them by performing an act of unconditional kindness to another. (Or don't – it's your life, your karma – you choose.)

43

When Dallalia Wilkins, petite one-time New Age con artiste, ex-aromatherapy healer, who found six million Swiss francs under a parked car in New Mexico and invested it in a Barcelona-based comedy troop that did so well she ended up being a top Broadway producer, arrived in Tenerife looking for Brandell Willard, on whom she'd had a burning crush for years, her hair was in a complete mess.

Without wasting a moment she walked straight into a new beachfront hair and beauty salon run by Uttlu Rormatage, who'd been fleeced of all his money in an expensive Australian divorce.

Sitting under the hairdryer having her nails done, she was suddenly overcome by the heat and went into a swoon. Out of the mists, smelling strongly of hairspray, a being appeared, (maybe an angel, maybe a barefoot doctor), who said,

'Haven't you learned yet, Wilkins, that stalking only ends in misery? The longing you feel is merely a disguised longing to be at one with your own spirit.'

'But I want him,' she replied like a spoilt child.

'It's not him, but the spirit within him you crave. That same spirit exists within you, Dallalia.' Whereupon he vanished through the holes in the hairdryer just as she came to.

Paying the bill and checking her new hairdo in the mirror, which wasn't at all bad for Tenerife, Dallalia wondered about accessing her spirit. Maybe that being had a point, she thought, and headed straight for the nearest beachfront bar, recently opened by Janko Poonanah, one-time West African doyen of Parisian haute couture who'd unsuccessfully attempted to destroy the world by adding sarin gas to his best-selling fragrance line, although it did wipe out two-thirds of the adult population of an economically insignificant developing country, and downed six gin and tonics in one go.

If you're caught in an unrequited love situation to the point of stalking your love object halfway round the world, affirm until you feel you could mean it: 'I no longer need waste time, money and energy searching for the unobtainable as a way to avoid real intimacy with someone available and suitable, unless I truly find it enjoyable and nurturing. I'm free to drop the obsession any time I like now!'

44

Glednel Jiltch, beret-sporting nuclear terrorist with extensive contacts in South America, the Middle East and Koh Samui, had always wanted to be a player in the global media scene. So when the opportunity arose to publish a youth-orientated glossy lifestyle magazine in hard copy and on the net, catering to the intelligent, spiritually-orientated, environmentally aware, mid- to high-income sector of the market, he jumped at it with both feet.

He left his personal assistant to handle a new shipment of tactical nuclear devices and thermo-barbaric bombs, instructing him to detonate a relatively harmless neutron bomb on the runway at Schipol airport in Holland for decoy purposes and to keep the authorities on their toes, and set straight to work on building the right team.

His first choice for editor was his snappily dressed childhood bisexual lover, Rivero Sambation, one-time professional taxidermist, now practising as a psychic tarot reader at a shop-front premises in Brighton on the UK's south coast.

Making it clear from the start that he would retain overall editorial control, Jiltch strongly suggested that the first issue's theme be power yoga around the world, as this would justify the disproportionately big sums of sponsorship money he was receiving from his power yoga tool company and thus augment his complex inter-national offshore tax structure and money-laundering operations.

Sambation knew what he was getting into, but you don't argue with a man who has his own tac-tical nuclear and thermo-barbaric arsenal, so, wasting no time, he called an editorial meeting with his new team. After twelve and a quarter solid hours' brainstorming, having exhausted every power yoga lead they had, it was decided that Sambation himself would go to the semi-arid desert island of Gomera to cover the power yoga retreat of the moment, being taught by Placentia Ordanato, the ravishing beauty who used to hold all New York and London in the palm of her hand.

Leaving his psychic tarot consultancy to a locum and reassuring Jiltch that all was in order,

Rivero set off on the first charter flight to Tenerife from Gatwick. Surprised when the flight attendant turned out to be an old flame, he didn't hesitate for a moment when she beckoned him into the toilets aft. Arranging themselves deftly within the confined space so as to enable them to fall into a wild *soixante-neuf* embrace, it was not possible for her to refrain from clamping down when the plane unexpectedly lurched.

As Sambation emitted a primal roar, part rage, part terror, a being, (maybe an angel, maybe a barefoot doctor), emerged from the paper towel dispenser and said, 'You blow too easy with the wind, Sambation. This trauma will snap you back into yourself.'

'She's bitten off my manhood and you're telling me to look on the bright side?!' he shouted, but the being had already disappeared down the used paper towel repository.

Sambation awoke a while later in post-op at the surprisingly well-equipped hospital on Tenerife, just as the doctor came in to assure him through an interpreter that his glans, which the flight crew had had enough prescience to freeze, was now successfully rejoined to his manhood, but that he would be best advised to abstain from unprotected sex till the stitches had dissolved and things were fully healed down there.

Don't wait for someone to bite off your body parts before waking up to who you really are and expressing yourself clearly to others, no matter how powerful or daunting they seem at the time. Centre yourself now by placing your palms one on either side of your pubic bone and, feeling the warmth penetrate, affirm with conviction: 'I remember exactly who I am and am now able to express that clearly to everyone.'

45

Janko Poonanah, one-time West African doyen of Parisian haute couture with his jaunty look and trademark blue fez, who had attempted unsuccessfully to destroy the developed world by adding sarin gas to his top-selling fragrance line and merely succeeded in killing off two-thirds of the adult population of a minor developing country, which warranted a nine-line article on the back page of a national newspaper, and who'd gone on to open a Tenerife beachfront bar called Janko's, looked up from the glasses he was cleaning as a petite, small but sexy-mouthed, slightly broken-nosed woman with a tidy new hairdo walked confidently into the bar, and felt something stir inside.

Dallalia Wilkins, petite one-time New Age con artiste, ex-aromatherapy healer, now successful Broadway producer hot on the trail of her long-term obsession, Brandell Willard, who had run off with Placentia Ordanato, who once held all New

York and London in the palm of her hand, to run a power yoga retreat on the semi-arid desert island of Gomera, had seen Janko's type before. Big, swarthy alpha male who'd tasted the good life, escaping the rat race by opening a bar on the beach. She thought she'd give him a wide berth. But something inside her stirred as he looked up from cleaning glasses and their eyes met.

After only a few moments of preliminary banter Poonanah closed the bar and walked arm in arm with Wilkins to the nearby harbour where they boarded his powerboat and set off on a pleasure trip round the island, not noticing the storm warnings.

When the big wave came that capsized the boat Dallalia freed herself from their impassioned embrace just in time to avoid sharing the fate of her new-found lover, who ended up being shredded to death on the propeller.

Instead she swallowed a lungful of water. As she sank, unconscious, to the cold sea bed, a being appeared, (maybe an angel, maybe a barefoot doctor, maybe a medium size squid – she couldn't tell), who said, 'I know you're probably thinking you can't hold onto a man. But don't worry about that one. He was a no-good son of a gun. He deserved what he got. Stop looking for fulfillment in love and love will come to you.'

'What good's that advice now I'm drowning?' she asked incredulously, thinking the being quite insensitive, but he'd already disappeared into the murky ocean depths. Suddenly a passing dolphin wearing a blue fez noticed Dallalia, scooped her up by her bra-strap and conveyed her swiftly to the surface and back to shore where, coughing and spluttering, she vomited up the sea water and walked back to town to tidy up.

If you've ignored the storm warnings and found your-self mangled on the propellers of life, don't give up. Connect to the source of all life, deep inside and ask for deliverance. Affirm: 'I am always delivered back to safety if I'm bold enough to believe it.'

46

Silphyre Treschulon had never wanted to be a sheep farmer. She'd always seen herself as a lady of leisure, but when her entire family was wiped out by an unexpected hurricane, she had no choice but to resign from the social circuit of London, Paris, New York, the Hamptons and Baden Baden and return to the family farm in Shropshire.

Life in the rainy countryside was dull. Night after night, Silphyre would sit alone knitting and indulging her hobby as a ham radio operator, occasionally managing to jam the local RAF nuclear attack early warning system, but otherwise feeling bored and restless most of the time. So it was without hesitation that she accepted the offer of the kindly CIA operative who phoned one day out of the blue, asking if she'd be willing to replace their field operative who'd gone AWOL, whose job it had been to spy on London. In exchange for this they would send a qualified sheep-farming team to take care of things while she was at work.

One night, carrying an attaché case full of stolen classified documents near Leicester Square after a particularly close shave where she'd almost been tumbled by the authorities, she felt a pressure headache coming on. She walked into a 24-hour pharmacy to pick up some painkillers and swallowed two immediately.

The man from the press who'd been trailing her all day couldn't believe his luck when Treschulon developed an allergic reaction and started convulsing on the shop floor. He wasted no time grabbing her case and making off with it into the night.

By the time the ambulance came, she had given herself concussion by banging the back of her head repeatedly on the floor and was seeing stars, one of which appeared to be a being, (maybe an angel, maybe a barefoot doctor), who said, 'You're a crazy bitch, but I like your fighting spirit. Remember you create your own reality. You no longer need live your life in reaction to others.'

When she came to, the being was gone and so was her attaché case. So, in fact, was her usefulness to the CIA, who, when the story broke in the morning papers, asked her to go underground for a while and suggested the semi-arid desert island of Gomera where she'd be well out of the limelight till all this blew over. They, in return, would maintain the sheep-farming team in place at her family farm till she got back.

She agreed instantly and in no time was being driven at top speed to Gatwick to board the first flight out to Tenerife, from where she was to catch the ferry over to Gomera.

If you feel like you're being tossed hither and thither by the storms of life, stop for one moment and pick a direction. Then go that way come what may. Say, 'I choose my own direction and however random my path may appear, my direction remains steady, my direction remains steady.'

✦

47

Klekenko Wallis was no ordinary girl so when she told her husband she was quitting the suburbs for good to pursue her life's queer dream of facilitating an internet start-up company in a sluggish market, he took her at her word.

When she arrived in New York however, she was approached on Fifth Avenue by a scout for a top international modelling agency, who'd instantly seen the potential in her alluring qualities and symmetrical features, and within a week had signed a multi-million dollar contract with an international cosmetics company.

Sitting in first class on a flight to London, Klekenko met Glednel Jiltch, beret-sporting nuclear terrorist with extensive contacts in South America, the Middle East and even Koh Samui, who, following a lifelong fascination with the media, had set up a glossy lifestyle magazine in hard copy format and on the net. He was instantly taken by her charm, poise and the turn of her ankle and noticing she was no ordinary girl invited her to winter with him on his yacht in the Maldives.

Driving to the jetty to pick up the launch after many hours travelling and one too many drinks, Klekenko jumped jauntily from the jeep, mistakenly assuming it had stopped when in fact it was still moving at a healthy seventy kilometres an hour, causing herself minor concussion and a bleeding bump at the back of her head as she went tumbling backwards on the hot tarmac.

Later, sitting sheepishly on the sun deck of Jiltch's yacht, feeling stupid and clumsy, wondering where it had all gone wrong, a being appeared out of the foam, (maybe an angel, maybe a barefoot doctor), who said, 'Embarrassment, Klekenko, is the nearest thing to bliss.'

'What do you mean?' she asked bewildered.

'It's an ecstatic state. Surrender to it for the adventure then move on, and don't waste a moment doubting the choices you made that got you here.'

'Uh?' she inquired, but the being had already vanished into the ocean swell.

Pulling herself together, she bade farewell to

Jiltch at the next port of call, explaining she had things to do and promised to be in touch.

Catching a plane to Frankfurt, she set to work immediately on facilitating her internet start-up company, which, bucking all the trends, did so well she was able to float within six months, netting her an undisclosed fortune. Some of this she used to settle out of court for breaking her modelling contract and the rest she spent on luxuries and treats she'd been denying herself for too long, including buying that beachfront bar she'd always wanted, eventually settling on one that had recently come unexpectedly onto the market in Tenerife called Janko's, which she immediately renamed Klekenko's.

Sometimes you need to mess yourself up a bit before you can come back to centre. At these times, affirm: 'Even when I'm messing myself up, I am perpetuating my own good.' For as you believe, so will it be.

48

Ushash Renpet, commercial house DJ at the pinnacle of his profession, and MC Chipploe Muhunzalez had been working as a team for two years before they discovered they both had a secret passion for the mobile telecommunications industry.

Deciding to invest the not inconsiderable record company revenues they'd gained during the heady days just before MP3 sent the industry into a nosedive, they bought into a local network and before long found themselves in the middle of a highly advantageous hostile takeover bid situation which not only netted them a few billion on paper overnight, but also effectively put them at the helm of the largest mobile network in Europe.

What fascinated them most was the unique opportunity to do Pan-European live DJ and MC sets over mobile networks.

However, unbeknownst to Ushash, Chipploe

had discovered religion and his lyrical content began to reflect that. At first it was subtle – the simple wearing of a diamante crucifix – but soon he was blatantly assuming the apocalyptic position to the extent that vast swathes of customers within the network coverage zone were becoming existentially despondent.

As share prices were wiped out overnight and Ushash sat with Chipploe trying to take stock, trying hard not to blame Chipploe for his sudden reversal of fortunes, a being appeared in the trail of smoke from the heroin he was inhaling and said, 'This is what happens when you loose touch with your artistic roots and start messing around with running global corporations. Maybe it's time to go back to the clubs and play some tunes for the ordinary people. Leave mobile telecommunications to the people who do that sort of thing and start having fun again.'

'But what am I going to do about his apocalyptic position?' asked Ushash, brushing a fleck of aluminium foil from the sleeve of his red satin jacket.

'Oh, yeah,' replied the being and, turning his attention to Chipploe, appeared in the Bible that he was clutching feverishly, from between the pages concerning the Revelations of St John.

'Chipploe, if you want to reach the people, drop all that holy-rollin' routine,' said the being, taking a bit of a chance. 'Try instead to talk in parables like other great masters who have gone before. It's much more effective in getting your message across.'

'What did he tell you?' Ushash later asked his friend.

'Oh, I dunno man, but maybe we should think of going back on the road and playing our tunes for the ordinary people,' Chipploe replied.

'Hallelulia!' Ushash exclaimed, and got on the phone to their bookings agent who booked them a low-key tour of southern Europe and the Canaries, including three nights at a relatively obscure, newly re-opened Tenerife beachfront bar called Klekenko's.

If you've been alienating your friends and followers recently by being a bit too pious, try taking yourself back to the roots that predate organized thought and divesting yourself of any notions you may have of being special. Be ordinary. Affirm: 'In my ordinariness will be found my salvation.'

49

Brandell Willard, one-time suicidal depressive, ex-drugs mule and con man, recently head of a rubber and fetishwear manufacturer and distributor on Seventh Avenue, now running a power yoga retreat on the semi-arid desert island of Gomera, taught by his lover, Placentia Ordanato, who used to hold all of New York and London in the palm of her hand, and with whom he'd run away to escape the clutches of Dallalia Wilkins who'd had an extreme crush on him for ages, realized the retreat was on to a winner as he watched all the unusually colourful and larger-than-life guests roll up.

Congratulating himself on a successful PR and marketing campaign which appeared to have instigated a genuine word-of-mouth buzz about the retreat, he decided to leave Placentia to handle the guests and to take the short ferry ride over to Tenerife, find a congenial beachfront bar and get plastered to relieve the tension while there was time.

Wandering into a newly re-opened bar called Klekenko's, formerly Janko's, run by Klekenko Wallis, the one-time suburban housewife turned successful model, now head of a fast-expanding internet start-up company, he was amazed to see the fabled DJs Ushash Renpet and MC Chipploe Muhunzalez doing a live set.

Brandell hadn't tied one on for ages and was only one tequila away from throwing up all over the floor by the time Rivero Sambation, snappily dressed one-time professional taxidermist, ex-psychic tarot reader, now editor of a glossy new lifestyle magazine owned by beret-sporting nuclear terrorist, Glednel Jiltch, wandered into the bar after being released from the surprisingly well-equipped Tenerife hospital where he'd just had his glans sewn back on after it was accidentally bitten off by a flight attendant in the toilet on the plane on the way over.

Sambation had no idea of the effect his words would have when he asked Brandell what he was drinking and was surprised when downing this, his seventeenth tequila, Brandell span on his heel once, keeled over, cracked his head on the edge of a marble-topped table and died instantly, thus prematurely ending a highly speckled career.

Just then, Dallalia Wilkins, petite ex-New Age con artiste, one-time aromatherapy healer, who'd wisely invested six million Swiss francs she'd found in a case under a parked car in New Mexico and had become a successful Broadway producer, and who'd had a burning obsession for Brandell for years, stumbled into the bar in a semi-state of shock after recently losing her new-found lover, Janko Poonanah, who'd owned the bar before Klekenko, when he was shredded by the propeller of his own powerboat after it capsized while taking her out on a pleasure trip round the island.

Seeing Brandell lying bloodied and senselessly dead on the floor without any warning compounded the impact of recent events. Suddenly it was all too much for her and she collapsed in a swoon, whereupon a being appeared, (maybe an angel, maybe a barefoot doctor), who said, 'It's what I keep telling you about the intransigence of all form. Every time you cling to someone, your attachment will cause suffering,' then disappeared as she awoke to the aroma of smelling salts being wafted under her nose by Sambation, who always carried such things in the inside pocket of his jacket in case of emergency.

She took one look at his come-to-bed eyes that hinted at hidden depths, and although she was in the midst of undeniable grief, she nevertheless fell uncontrollably, irredeemably in love (again).

If you've been tying one on to the point of dizziness, resist the next glass, as it's always more prudent to remain in command of your body if you wish to prevent senseless untimely death. Instead affirm: 'I need no longer blot out the majesty of my moment-to-moment existence with sedatives of any kind. I am willing to experience being here without artificial aids, at least for a moment or two.'

✦

50

After his heated dealings with key members of the Northern Wa along the Burmese border, Menxrano Kwappsia, ex-head of a large global accountancy company, recently charged with fraud in New York and also suspected of being at the centre of a vast money-laundering operation involving the late notorious underworld figure Rits Historìco, was hiding out in Thailand under an assumed identity till the heat died down, and was feeling pretty shaken up.

Though the downtown bar and restaurant business he'd bought for cash was thriving, he was suffering from tropical torpor and was contemplating his next move – a season in London teaching master classes to concert pianists, a spell in the north country writing that poetry book he'd been promising himself to do for years, or getting involved in internet-related crime in Cambodia – he just couldn't make up his mind.

As he usually did when in the midst of such quandaries, he went for a trek in the jungle to clear his head, uncharacteristically forgetting to factor in the possibility of mosquito-born malaria.

Lying tossing and turning, sweating and yellow-faced in hospital one week later, painfully impaled on the horns of his dilemma, a being appeared, (maybe an angel, maybe a barefoot doctor) out of the mists of his delirium, who, gambling in vain that a push in the wrong direction might cause a polarity reaction and produce a pull in the right direction from within said, 'It really doesn't matter, Menxrano. Why not go for the internet-related crime in Cambodia? At least it will get your adrenaline going and the money'll be far better.'

Two weeks later, having handed over the running of the business to a local Thai, knowing he was going to get robbed but factoring in a few percentage points to cover it, he set off for upland Cambodia. Deep in the tribal warfare zone, in a rudimentary hut on stilts, he booted up his top-of-the-line laptop and using infra-red send to his mobile phone, logged on and started work.

Within hours, millions of yen having been deftly diverted to a secret account in Liechtenstein,

Menxrano strolled outside for a smoke, still quite weak from the malaria, tripped on a loose step and fell onto the upturned blade of a scythe which had been carelessly left on the ground by a drunk local farmer, and was instantly decapitated.

If you find yourself impaled on the horns of a dilemma, don't lose your head over it. Simply wait and in a short while everything will come to pass exactly as it was always going to anyway. Why worry? Affirm: 'Every day I am becoming better at not trying to outguess the future.' In this present moment everything you need to know will be revealed.

✦

51

When an email brought news of the death of his old friend Menxrano Kwappsia by accidental self-decapitation in upland Cambodia, occasional freelance journalist Chevrie Hamptu, once defrocked priest Pefflon Isissies before he'd changed his name by deed poll and started a new life, was already on the ferry nearing the semi-arid desert island of Gomera to cover a story on the power yoga retreat taught by Placentia Ordanato, who used to hold all New York and London in the palm of her hand.

His lover, Sewwepta Conchaxto, dark, curly-haired, half-gypsy travelling futures trader, who'd been on her way to a prestigious new job in Frankfurt and a life of luxury with wealthy play-boy, Franz Bisch, when she met Hamptu in Amsterdam while he was on a drugs binge, and had decided on a whim to accompany him on his assignment instead, showed little concern as he deleted the email on his mobile phone and broke down weeping on the ferry's upper deck.

Through the blur of his tears, Hamptu thought he saw a being, (maybe an angel, maybe a barefoot doctor), who said consolingly, 'There is no death, Hamptu, only change and transformation, you could even say resurrection. Menxrano Kwappsia lives, my friend. Celebrate that,' then vanished as soon as Hamptu's eyes had cleared.

By the time their taxi pulled up at the mountainside finca where the power yoga retreat was being held, things were beginning to wear a bit thin between him and Sewwepta. He barely managed to conceal his interest in Placentia, who was sobbing as she swept down the narrow staircase towards them, followed by the two policemen who'd come to inform her of the unfortunate accidental death of her lover Brandell Willard, large-eared and unruly featured one-time suicidal depressive, ex-drugs mule and con man, most recently head of a rubber and fetishwear manufacturer and distributor on Seventh Avenue, who, until cracking his head on a marble-topped table in Klekenko's Tenerife beachfront bar while tying one on and dying instantly, was running the marketing and administration of the retreat.

Through her tears, Placentia, a ravishing beauty who had once held all of New York and London in the palm of her hand, and who had developed a keen eye for these things, noticed the glint in Hamptu's eye and found it strangely comforting.

Though the thought of the death of your loved ones or yourself may alarm you, be assured that death is a perfectly natural part of the life-cycle, perhaps the most natural, and as such you're innately equipped to accommodate it. When it eventually happens to someone close to you you'll handle it far better than you could imagine now. By the same token, let your fear remind you of how precious others are to you and make sure you share some sacred loving time together while you still have the opportunity.

52

DJ Ushash Renpet and MC Chipploe Muhunzalez, having reached the pinnacle of their careers, subsequently invested their fortunes in mobile telecommunications, leading to their being at the helm of the largest mobile network in Europe, only to discover that they were losing touch with their fans. Now they wanted their London headquarters redecorated after returning from a short tour of southern Europe where they shared their music with the ordinary people and there was only one choice: Trevylon Drummahk, by some accounts the most popular paint finisher and gilding expert in all Hong Kong.

In the 1990s, at the age of 43, Trevylon Drummahk had gone from his native Swansea in South Wales to Hong Kong on an interior design job, just before the territory was handed back to the Chinese, had fallen in love with the young daughter of a factory owner who had turned out to be a Russian operative just out to garner gilding secrets, and had left him after he'd divulged his technique to her, yet he'd stayed on in Hong Kong anyway, having grown accustomed to the smell of the place. After receiving the call, he walked slowly, head bowed, to the beach. The day was hot, airless and humid.

At first, Drummahk was stunned. Renpet and Muhunzalez were not exactly small fry. Wondering if he wasn't biting off more than he could chew, he became anxious. Anxiety gave way to fear. Fear gave way to anger. Anger gave way to self-pity and self-pity triggered the existential can of worms he'd been trying to deny for so long. It was with a heavy cloud hanging over his head that he now stepped on to the beach.

His first thought was to walk into the sea and just keep walking till he drowned.

'This'll show them that there's more to Trevylon Drummahk than paint-finishing and gilding!' he thought, as the waves lapped about his ears.

Choking on salt-water, strands of seaweed caught in his hair, he coughed, spluttered and threw up the bacon and eggs he'd just breakfasted on. Just as he was about to go under, a being (maybe an angel, maybe a barefoot doctor), poked his head out through the patch of vomit floating on the water.

'Let's stop and look at what's going on here for moment, Drummahk,' he suggested. 'Because you've never had the time or inclination to look at yourself in depth, you've been operating an avoidance strategy while pinning your sense of identity on your work as a paint finisher and gilding expert, which will obviously wear a bit thin from time to time. The existential disturbance you're experiencing is no more permanent than this vomit. You can let it go the same way. Remember, Drummahk, behind all disturbance lies your immortal spirit and nothing can diminish that even were you never to pick up a paintbrush again. You're innately magnificent, Drummahk. And now, if you're feeling a little clearer, I think there's a job waiting for you, is there not?' he asked rhetorically, before vanishing.

Swimming the short distance back to shore with new resolve, Trevylon dried off in the sun and headed straight for the airport to catch the first flight to London.

The job turned out so well that he soon became the talk of London and Paris and it wasn't long before he was invited to decorate the mountain hideout on the semi-arid desert island of Gomera of Silphyre Treschulon, one-time sheep farmer and CIA field operative, previously assigned to spy on London, but now gone to ground till the heat blew over after she'd lost a bundle of sensitive stolen official documents which had found their way into the tabloid press.

Making a concerted effort not to let success go to his head, however, Drummahk never returned her call.

If you feel like you're living your life as a surface-only affair, stop and affirm: 'At the very core of me, I am an immortal spirit without bounds or limits and no matter what occurs in my surface reality I am innately mag-nificent – always have been, always am and always will be!'

53

Being a professional part-time diving superintendent and often having to dive herself, while going for her doctorate in artificial intelligence, was beginning to take its toll on Desdakita Polonto. Her close friends and associates were starting to notice odd quirks appearing, typical of those who plumb the depths too frequently.

But Polonto, dark-skinned, green-eyed and by no means unattractive, half-Irish, half-Punjabi and consumed with culture conflict, was driven by internal demons that wouldn't let her rest for a moment. When she received a call offering her a six-week job laying optical fibre in the polluted waters off the Mumbai shoreline, she jumped at it.

As she'd feared, however, it turned out to be another of those low-budget, poorly equipped outfits so prevalent in modern times. On the third day out, at a depth of 60 metres, the old garden hosepipe which carried her sole air supply collapsed from the pressure, causing her to swallow far more than the recommended amount of water-born Mumbai effluent, which travelled swiftly to her liver, suddenly compounding the pre-menstrual migraine she was nursing.

'That's it, I've had enough,' she screamed internally, stamping her flipper-clad foot on the seabed and making for the surface far above, with all her might.

'This is the worst case of the bends and unrelated liver poisoning syndrome I've ever seen!' exclaimed the consultant on the sweaty hospital ward that same afternoon. 'I doubt she'll ever recover her sanity,' he half-mumbled to a junior doctor as he turned away to attend another patient.

Although she couldn't get his dialect, Polonto could tell from the tone of his voice that the prognosis wasn't good and fell instantly into a sharp emotional decline.

From the deep recesses of her inner turmoil, appeared a being, (maybe an angel, maybe a barefoot doctor), who said, 'Don't take the opinions of others as anything more than opinions. Beyond opinions lies a realm where the power to heal yourself is simply a choice you make. Choose it now Polonto and you will be healed!' Whereupon he passed his hand once over her body, blew hard in her left ear and vanished.

Suddenly springing from her bed, ripping the drip from her arm and hurriedly signing a disclaimer, she ran from the hospital in her bed clothes and stopping only long enough to withdraw some cash, hailed a cab to the airport and caught the first flight home. There she set immediately to work on her doctorate, which was so well received she was offered a place at MIT working at the forefront of human-machine interface issues.

However, throughout this time, her out-of-work actor boyfriend, Hyppollite Rogers, a ruddy-faced, devil-may-care loose cannon at the best of times, had become inexplicably possessive and on reaching boiling point had invested the last of his savings on paying two unsavoury types to abduct her and effectively imprison her in a disused rehearsal space he happened to be renting above Klekenko's Tenerife beachfront bar.

If you're worried about your mental or physical health, stop now and be willing to accept that at the deepest level, the big YOU inside chooses whether to be healthy or sick, whether to live or die. Allow your thoughts to settle now. Let your breathing slow down and deepen. Withdraw your awareness into the centre of your brain and with love flowing from your heart declare boldly: 'I choose health now!'

54

When Zank Drazdan III, ex-CIA field operative previously spying on London till he got in over his head and was forced to run off to the semi-arid desert island of Gomera to start afresh and maybe write that novel he'd always had in him, disembarked from the Tenerife ferry, he felt instantly crestfallen. There was something gloomy, foreboding and godforsaken about the place he couldn't put his finger on.

Suddenly beset by an existential attack tantamount to a nervous breakdown, he sat down against the harbour wall and began to weep. The tears fell in torrents, his chest heaved and before long he was catharting like a mad person undergoing Reichian therapy.

In that altered state between wailing and howling, observed wryly by a group of waiting taxidrivers and other amused onlookers, he thought he saw a being (maybe an angel, maybe a barefoot doctor), walking on the harbour water towards him with outstretched arms, calling, 'Zank, Zank, Zank – do not be dismayed, I haven't forsaken you.'

'But this place you guided me to ...' sobbed Drazdan, 'I trusted you. I trusted your taste ...' he gestured with his hand at his surroundings, appearing to the taxi-drivers and other onlookers like a mad person talking to the air.

'I know, it's a dump,' acceded the being, surveying the sombre scenery. 'Forgive me, buddy, I'm afraid even beings get it wrong sometimes. I've had all kinds of peoples' dramas to deal with lately. Look, how about Koh Samui? I can get you a good deal ...'

'Koh Samui!?' Zank retorted, 'Any charm that place may once have had has long been destroyed by the destructive forces of low-rent mass-tourism – and the nightlife's dire.'

'Palma de Majorca?' tried the being one last time.

'Nah,' replied Zank dejectedly.

'Well, you know Zank, I could just tell you to get lost and find your own goddamn hideaway, you ungrateful bastard. Authors – you're all the same – bunch of spoilt children! But I'm a kindly being and won't descend so low. Look around you now and say, "I am king of no matter what!" six times and your nightmare will be instantaneously transformed into a dream.'

At which the being spun round, sprinted off across the harbour water and disappeared behind a passing tug that was towing an upturned powerboat with what looked like human remains stuck to its propellers.

Zank repeated the words and suddenly felt expunged of his torment. He picked himself up, dusted himself down and wasted no time jumping on the next ferry back to Tenerife, where he stopped to touch up the colour on his fake goatee at a beachfront hair salon run by Uttlu Rormatage, failed suicide, who'd lost everything in an Australian divorce finally to pursue his dream as a hairdresser, who on feeling a certain empathy with Drazdan, gave him the address of a safe house in upland Catalunya near the Pyrenees where he'd be able to write his novel in peace, and the phone number of a good London literary agent for when the time came.

As soon as the dye on his goatee was dry, Zank didn't waste a second in jumping on the first flight out to Barcelona, where, renting an economy class car, he drove straight to an undisclosed address in the foothills and began writing without delay.

Sometimes it's as if your guides have left you. They haven't – they're just pushing you to seek spiritual guidance from your own self and remember what you already know. Affirm: 'No one knows the answer better than I myself. From now on, I, as a multi-dimensional, universal being, am prepared to be my own spiritual guide and take responsibility for it. Wherever and however I find myself, is exactly where and how I'm meant to be right now!'

55

When Dunkalini Unga, prima ballerina and former Capoeira student of daring, dashing Brazilian
champion, Nervo Nergal, now turned roof-
thatching technician, arrived at the semi-arid
desert island of Gomera mountainside finca where
Placentia Ordanato, ravishing beauty who used to
hold all New York and London in the palm of her
hand, was teaching a power yoga retreat, she was
surprised to find Sewwepta Conchaxto, dark curly-
haired travelling half-gypsy futures trader, whom
she'd once met travelling in India during her gap
year, sitting alone in the lobby heaving with sobs.

Falling into each others arms and shrieking
as only girls who met in India on their gap year
do, Sewwepta poured out her story. How she'd
forsaken a prestigious new job in Frankfurt and a
life of luxury with wealthy playboy, Franz Bisch,
to follow new-found lover, occasional freelance
journalist Chevrie Hamptu, previously defrocked

priest Pefflon Isissies before he'd changed his name by deed poll, whom she'd hooked up with while he was on a drugs binge in Amsterdam and who was covering the retreat for Reuters, and who had fallen into an impassioned tryst with Ordanato only an hour after their arrival. What rankled her most, she explained, though she didn't know why herself, was hearing Ordanato screaming in ecstasy from her bedroom, 'Pefflon, oh, Pefflon!'

As Dunkalini stroked her friend's cheek in an attempt to console her, a being, (maybe an angel, maybe a barefoot doctor, maybe just an astral voyeur), appeared to them both as if from thin air and said, 'Girls, girls! The drama will unfold according to its own blueprint. Trust that the consciousness that created that blueprint is benevolent.'

'Uh?' Dunkalini and Sewwepta muttered in unison.

'I'm simply saying look on the bright side. This shift of dynamics leaves space for something new to occur – something even better.'

Suddenly, as if from nowhere, both girls were swept up in an unexpected, seemingly random tidal wave of desire and, looking searchingly into each other's eyes, realized what each had known all along but hadn't been able to acknowledge until now, and without a moment's hesitation fell into an uninhibited embrace.

Sometimes it takes a shock for you to recognize the blessing that was in front of your nose all the while. Take a deep breath while considering all the blessings that surround you now and as you exhale, affirm: 'I am now open to all the blessings that life holds for me.'

56

Nervo Nergal, daring, dashing Brazilian Capoeira champion, childhood sweetheart of Salbinellas Marina, who'd killed Salbinellas' lover, notorious underworld figure Rits Historìco and his minder, Capstan, with a simple kick to the temple, but who'd gone into a decline in the hinterlands of Bahia when Salbinellas left him for the second time in his life to sell SoHo loft conversions, was fairly stunned on walking into the lobby of the mountainside finca on the semi-arid desert island of Gomera where Placentia Ordanato, who once held all New York and London in the palm of her hand, was teaching a power yoga retreat, to find his former Capoeira pupil, prima ballerina turned roof-thatching technician, Dunkalini Unga, naked, with hair dishevelled, in the arms of similarly disposed Sewwepta Conchaxto, and wasted no time insinuating himself into the action.

Tossed on a stormy sea of undulating female

body parts, nearing the point of no return, his ardour was only momentarily dampened by shock when the finca door opened and in walked Salbinellas arm in arm with her lover, New York senator Porphyry Trents, one-time bigwig in Scottish politics, who, after breaking her spine in three places attempting the triple while indulging her dream of being a flying trapeze artiste, miraculously recovered and was discovered by Hollywood, becoming a star of circus films and ending up as a bigwig in American politics, whose copybook was blotted only by the deaths of floppy-haired retro rock band HT Russell while playing a gig on a platform suspended between two downtown Manhattan skyscrapers, whose exact location was kept secret for obvious reasons.

His basic Brazilian *joie de vivre* and eye for the main chance did not let him wilt for long, however, and in no time, using nothing more than clear intent and abundant charm, he had orchestrated things to also accommodate Salbinellas and Porphyry, who, feeling liberated from the pressures of work, were glad to strip off and join them on the cool flagstone floor.

The moans, squeals, grunts and groans emanating from the lobby below woke Placentia

Ordanato from her post-coital slumber, and without disturbing her new lover Chevrie Hamptu, she stole downstairs to see what was happening.

The sight of the writhing mass of bodies on the cool flagstone floor gave her a start. In that instant appeared a being (maybe an angel, maybe a barefoot doctor), who said, 'Looks like the retreat has an agenda of its own. Wisdom consists of riding with what is, enhancing it where possible as you go,' and promptly disappeared.

Placentia hesitated for only a moment to ponder the relevance of power yoga before removing her towelling bathrobe and joining the affray.

Do you sometimes feel you're simply following the crowd? Occasionally following the crowd brings you fulfillment. Usually it won't. Affirm: 'I only follow my own path and whoever wants to walk the same way is welcome (as long as they're not a nuisance).'

57

When Harvard Arequipa, silver-haired lawyer for the estate of notorious underworld figure, the late Rits Historìco, killed along with his minder Capstan by a simple kick to the temple delivered by daring, dashing Brazilian Capoeira champion, Nervo Nergal, arrived on Tenerife looking for a woman who'd made off with an expensive Italian attaché case filled with six million of his late client's Swiss francs from under a parked car in New Mexico, he began to wonder why he'd ever listened to the advice of that psychic tarot reader, Rivero Sambation, and gone to Gomera.

Wandering into Klekenko's beachfront bar he was put off-balance to see Rivero in the arms of a small but sexy-mouthed, slightly broken-nosed woman. Paying scant attention to the medics wheeling out the corpse of one Brandell Willard, who had just met an untimely accidental death while tying one on, Arequipa strolled straight over to the smooching couple and demanded, 'What the hell are you doing here, Sambation?'

Before Rivero had had time to explain how he'd been taken on as editor of beret-sporting nuclear terrorist Glednel Jiltch's new glossy lifestyle magazine, and was just on his way to Gomera to cover a power yoga story, Harvard's goat was up. Releasing all his pent-up frustration at having had to fly economy to Tenerife, he punched Sambation hard in the crotch.

Not realizing that Sambation, who had just been released from the surprisingly well-equipped local hospital, where his glans had just been sewn back on after an incident involving an old flame in the toilet of the plane over from Gatwick, was wearing a cricket-style protective box, it took him by surprise to find all the knuckles of his right hand broken simultaneously.

As his nervous system started to fully register the extent of the pain and his vision began to blur a little, a being, (maybe an angel, maybe a barefoot doctor) appeared and said in an I-told-you-so tone of voice, 'Karma, silver-haired dude – simple cause and effect. Reap what you sow and so on.'

'Sow?!!...What?!!!' shouted Arequipa out loud, but the being had gone, leaving him to the puzzled stares of Sambation and his new-found lover, Dallalia Wilkins, petite one-time New Age con artiste, ex-aromatherapy healer, who'd found six million Swiss francs in an expensive Italian attaché case under a parked car in New Mexico and used it to invest in a Barcelona comedy troop that did so well she ended up being a top Broadway producer.

Suddenly Harvard broke down before them, screaming from pain and desperation, eventually calming down enough to explain to Dallalia, to whom he'd taken a bit of a shine, how he was looking for a woman who'd taken six million Swiss francs.

Listening sympathetically, Dallalia suddenly excused herself to powder her nose. Prising open the lavatory window she made off into the night just as up-and-coming experimental breaks DJ, Swink Taloon, looking for his lawyer, Harvard Arequipa, because he so desperately needed the advance for his new record, wandered in off the street by chance and, paying no attention to Arequipa's delicate state, immediately started nagging him to get on the phone to the record company. (DJs!)

Sometimes it's hard to strike the balance between nagging someone and being constructively persistent. First make your intent to achieve your aim as strong as steel. Second affirm: 'I deserve the help of others in achieving all aims that are in accord with the natural good of all.'

58

Dark-skinned, green-eyed, half-Irish, half-Punjabi, culturally torn, deeply driven Desdakita Polonto, one-time diving superintendent now working at the cutting edge of the human-machine interface at MIT after getting her doctorate in artificial intelligence, recently abducted by her devil-may-care, loose cannon boyfriend, Hyppolite Rogers, in a sudden fit of possessiveness and held captive in a disused rehearsal space he happened to be renting above Klekenko's Tenerife beachfront bar, had gone through the panic stage and had started to settle into her enforced captivity. Her abductors weren't such bad eggs – it was a living after all. She understood that drive.

Not that she'd given up hope of escape, and when she heard what she presumed was the lavatory window of the beachfront bar below being prised open she wasted no time in asking to be excused to attend to a call of nature. Opening the window she called out, 'Help!' through the iron grill to the woman beating a hasty escape down a back street.

Dallalia Wilkins, petite, small but sexy-mouthed, one-time New Age con artiste turned aromatherapy healer, who having made off with six million Swiss francs she'd found in an expensive Italian attaché case left under a parked car in New Mexico, had invested it in a Barcelona comedy troop that did so well she ended up being a top Broadway producer, but was now on the run from Harvard Arequipa, lawyer for the estate of the late Rits Històrico, notorious underworld figure, whose brief it was to retrieve that same six million Swiss francs belonging to his client's estate, heard the woman's cry for help but chose to ignore it.

Feeling suddenly dejected and slightly out of sorts, Desdakita started banging her head against the wall in desperation, eventually falling into a stupor and sinking slowly down onto the putrid lavatory floor. Staring into a stagnant puddle of unknown composition she thought she saw the face of a being, (maybe an angel, maybe a barefoot doctor), who said, 'Even solid walls and iron grills yield to the mind that is truly focused.'

At which, rising from the puddle to his full

height, he pulled the iron grill from its concrete bedding as easily as if he was shredding a piece of toilet paper and smiling in a what-a-clever-being-I-am sort of way, disappeared back into the puddle.

Desdakita wasted no time in squeezing herself through the narrow opening, jumping the fourteen feet down to ground level and charging up the back street. There, after rounding a corner, she bumped into Dallalia who was resting to catch her breath, looked her straight in the eye and said, 'Bitch!' as she slapped her hard on the cheek.

Next time you're up against an apparently unmovable obstruction, stop and focus your mind on attaining your goal. To help achieve this, hold the tip of your dominant forefinger seven to ten inches from your face and gaze at it in a concentrated fashion for nine minutes a day. This may not remove all obstructions to your progress immediately, but it will help focus your mind to a level of intensity that will surprise you and what's more, you'll get to know your own fingertip better.

59

When one-time reluctant rent-boy Bambassi Rongalon, unwittingly enmeshed in a secret service sex scandal involving a Chinese Politburo member, who'd fled to Tenerife until the heat died down and by chance had picked up a flyer advertising a power yoga retreat on the nearby semi-arid desert island of Gomera, walked into the lobby of the mountainside finca where the retreat was being held, it was not without some confusion.

Imagining power yoga to be something quite different, Bambassi was nonplussed to see the mass of writhing bodies lost in the throes of group sexual ecstasy on the cool flagstone floor.

Taking a moment to get his bearings after the long journey, he soon found himself reverting to old patterns and in no time had gone into the kitchen, stripped, and put on the spare French maid's outfit he found serendipitously hanging behind the kitchen door in case of emergencies.

Walking back into the lobby in his new attire, brandishing a tray of cocktails he'd thoughtfully just mixed, he handed out drinks, mingled a bit, and soon found himself compulsively offering to be a slave to Placentia Ordanato, ravishing beauty who once held all New York and London in the palm of her hand, but who was now holding the breast of Senator Porphyry Trents instead, and who to all intents and purposes was meant to be running the retreat.

Ordanato accepted his offer graciously. But now, sitting on the narrow staircase polishing her slingback stilettos, Bambassi was suddenly overcome by the futility of repeating the same old pattern again and again.

Climbing slowly to the head of the stairs and finding the trapdoor that led onto the gabled roof, he was just about to throw himself off into the valley far below, when a being appeared in the air before him, (maybe an angel, maybe a barefoot doctor, maybe a large mutant bird) who said, 'Wait, Rongalon! It's at these times when you feel like throwing in the towel that the change you've been craving occurs. Don't be down on yourself for acting out old unworkable patterns again and again compulsively. Simply observe yourself compassionately without prejudice and over time you will learn to override those same patterns effortlessly.'

Even though the full significance of the being's message was lost on Bambassi, whose education had been fairly limited and whose vocabulary did not extend to many of the being's more polysyllabic words, he felt an irrational but instinctive trust for the being and surrendering to what he could only describe as the pull of unconditional love, closed his weary eyes and fell helplessly into the being's arms, not realizing that the being had already vanished into thin air, and so went crashing over the precipice into the semi-arid valley below, dying on impact with a medium-sized volcanic rock.

When you're caught between a rock and a hard place, it's yourself you need to trust. If you find that difficult, repeat: 'I trust myself to deliver myself from all danger' 24 times before tomorrow.

60

Waking from his post-coital slumber at the power yoga retreat at the mountainside finca on the semi-arid desert island of Gomera, taught by Placentia Ordanato, the ravishing beauty who used to hold all New York and London in the palm of her hand, occasional freelance journalist Chevrie Hamptu – formerly defrocked priest Pefflon Isissies, before his name change by deed poll, who was covering the power yoga story for Reuters, and who had fallen into bed with Ordanato only a few moments after arrival, abandoning his companion, Sewwepta Conchaxto, to an orgy in the finca lobby – was shocked to see the headless ghost of his childhood friend Menxrano Kwappsia, who'd recently died by accidental self-decapitation in upland Cambodia, at the end of the bed.

Asking for an electronic organizer as his dis-combobulated state prevented him from vocalizing, Kwappsia's ghost typed in the details and pin number of the secret account in Liechtenstein to which he'd diverted the billions he'd made from internet-related crime, pressed 'save' and gradually dematerialized.

Stopping only long enough to grab his suitcase and call for a cab on his mobile, Hamptu pocketed the organizer and, walking stealthily past the writhing mass of bodies lost in the throes of sexual ecstasy on the cool flagstone floor of the finca lobby, jumped in the cab and took the first ferry over to Tenerife to catch a flight to Vienna.

Falling asleep on the plane, Hamptu dreamed he saw a being (maybe an angel, maybe a barefoot doctor), who said, 'Be sure to give between ten and fifteen per cent of your new-found fortune to a charity of your choice. That way you clear any negative energy attached to the money. Oh, and congratulations.'

When Hamptu awoke he'd forgotten the dream, but after transferring the account over to his local high-street branch for easier access and investing heavily in the largest mobile telecommunications network in Europe, run by DJ Ushash Renpet and MC Chipploe Muhunzalez, as well as a fast-growing, in spite of market conditions, internet start-up company owned by Klekenko Wallis, he flew on a whim to London and, walking randomly along Charing Cross Road, handed a suitcase filled with eight and half million euro in used notes to the first homeless person who asked him for some spare change.

After that he lived a fulfilled and contented life until he was crushed while skate-boarding a few months later by a freak rockslide in a park on the outskirts of Oslo, after reading, in an old club-culture magazine, an interview with Norwegian club promoter Bleckstrak Nengervan about his early years, which inspired Hamptu to conduct a simple experiment with reality and follow in his footsteps, or should that be skid marks?

There's no way to avoid freak rockslides and other such occurrences, so be sure to be as generous as you can to others during the time you have left, just so you don't die feeling mean-spirited. Affirm: 'The more I give, the more I receive. Every euro I spend returns to me multiplied.'

61

Sister Kimbal Neosho – unremarkable-looking ex-Buddhist nun, formerly Professo Expressional, loving relationships trainer turned Southern Baptist preacher before having a sex change after crashing his Oldsmobile into the tour bus of floppy-haired retro-rock band, HT Russell – and Drifto Continental – a local unshaven, wind-burnt drunk and divorce lawyer she'd hooked up with at a bar near the Californian Buddhist retreat she'd been running – walked into the power yoga retreat at the mountainside finca on the semi-arid desert island of Gomera, run by Placentia Ordanato, ravishing beauty who once held all New York and London in the palm of her hand, and taking one look at the mass of bodies writhing in the throes of indiscriminate group sexual ecstasy on the cool flagstone floor of the finca lobby, turned right around and jumping in the cab which they'd intuitively told to wait, made straight for the ferry back to the nearby island of Tenerife.

For Sister Neosho, it was just too soon after renouncing her vows to jump directly into the realms of group sex. At least that's how she justified it to herself. For Drifto it was just an adolescent complex about having a small penis and fat belly. Nursing cocktails now at Klekenko's beachfront bar, each sat reflecting on the troublesome personal issues thrown up by recent events.

'Why did you run away from the orgy?' asked Sister Neosho at last, cutting through the pregnant silence like a well-honed machete.

'To be honest, I've always had a complex about my dick being too small and having a fat belly,' replied Drifto candidly, 'and you?'

'Well, I told myself it was because of it being too soon after renouncing my vows, but to be perfectly frank, I used to be a man until I had a sex-change operation and was worried the scars would show,' replied Sister Neosho with equal candour.

Drifto seemed to notice Neosho's Adam's apple and large hands for the first time. He turned as green as a bottle of mouthwash and without stopping to settle the bill or grab his suitcase, ran to the beach and threw up with extreme force over an idle jetski-bike.

Sitting down with his face in his hands, wondering where to go from here, a being, (maybe an angel, maybe a barefoot doctor), appeared through the gaps between his fingers and said, 'This is just happening to let you know your drifting days are over, Drifto. It's time to put down some roots and devote your time to creating something useful for the world,' and promptly disappeared.

Without even taking a moment to wash the vomit from his face or drink a glass of water, Continental made straight for the airport and took the first flight out to anywhere, which oddly enough turned out to be to Portsmouth on the UK's south coast. There, signing on at a local recruitment agency, he took the first job that came up and went straight to work building missiles for an international arms manufacturer with a strong youth culture following, moonlighting evenings and weekends behind the bar of a pub in the centre of town to supplement his salary.

When events occur that throw your whole picture of reality into chaos, do not always rush to adjust your set. Allow yourself to remain in the chaotic state and shortly an entirely new path will reveal itself. Breathe in deeply and as you exhale, affirm: 'Out of chaos comes a new, improved direction.'

62

Snopme Chaddelow, once head of the biggest private security firm in Argentina before being busted for financing a large consignment of acid, now living back in his home town of Brighton on the UK's south coast but looking for a timeshare apartment or small villa on Tenerife, accosted on the street while on a date with Quimper Frondondo, demi-celebrity UK TV newsreader, by Lango Faldo, one-time world-famous spiritual teacher, ex-personal fitness trainer and failed family entertainment TV presenter, now selling timeshares, was only mildly disconcerted when Frondondo went off with Kwipstah Tonk, ex youth-marketing consultant, now activist, just escaped from gaol for scaling the wall of the local TV station. He gladly accepted Faldo's offer of a few drinks at Klekenko's beachfront bar where they could go through the timeshare contract for the small villa he'd chosen.

Just as Snopme was about to sign, Lango stayed his hand, saying, 'I can't let you do this.'

'Why? It's a perfectly good small villa and will suit my needs well,' replied Chaddelow bemusedly.

'Yes, but my heart's not in selling it to you. You see, I used to be a world-famous spiritual teacher, and I feel like I'm selling out on myself. Would you excuse me?' At which he got up suddenly and walked down to the harbour, where, dangling his feet in the murky polluted water, he hung his head and cried.

Through the rainbow hues of a small oil slick floating on the water, a being emerged, (maybe an angel, maybe a barefoot doctor), who after clearing the putrid water from his nostrils, said, 'Lango Faldo, one-time world-famous spiritual teacher, look what's become of you. You've scaled the heights and now you're plumbing the depths. It's all grist for the mill. Simply observe yourself experiencing the swing.'

'But I've lost touch with my original purpose. I don't know what I'm here for anymore,' he replied ruefully.

'Get back to the street, to where you started, Faldo. Now go on, be off with you.' And with that the being took a deep breath, re-submerged himself into the filthy harbour waters and disappeared.

Faldo wasted no time in jumping on the first plane to London. On arrival he made straight for Charing Cross Bridge and began preaching his original gospel, a bit rustily at first, but soon warming to his theme and attracting a huge crowd. In only a matter of weeks word had spread and his following grew faster than ever before, leading to a lucrative sponsorship deal with a global sports shoe manufacturer, netting him enough to retire to Koh Samui, where he settled, wasting no time in becoming a partial alcoholic, preaching the word to anyone drunk enough to listen.

Never lose sight of the pendulum's swing. As long as the pendulum keeps swinging, the adventure can progress. Affirm: 'I deserve to have anything I desire.' Saying that to yourself often enough can produce some pretty strange results in your life. Try it.

63

Kwipstah Tonk, one-time high-flying youth-marketing consultant turned activist, jailed in Tenerife for scaling the local TV station wall as part of a ETA fundraising stunt, who escaped when a 6.9 earthquake rocked the island and destroyed the gaol, leading him to run serendipitously into Quimper Frondondo, demi-celebrity UK news-reader and member of one of the noblest families in all Madrid, who'd bought a mountainside finca complete with torture dungeon on the nearby semi-arid desert island of Gomera as a weekend retreat, and who fell instantly in love with Kwipstah at first sight of the dust in his hair, prosthetic arm and newly mangled leg from a recently falling girder, had found himself initially enthralled.

But stretched out now on her digitally controlled rack, his mangled leg throbbing wildly and his armpits about to snap, Kwipstah was starting to question this whole falling in love at first sight business.

As Quimper keyed in a new value on her laptop and the rack stretched him just that bit too far for comfort, he barely managed to scream, 'Ease off, will you, babes!' before losing consciousness as his brachial plexii elongated past the point of no return.

From the dark recesses of his unconscious mind, a being materialized and said, 'The stretch will do you good, Tonk. It will serve to open up your heart centre. Once the heart centre opens and your capacity to give and receive unconditional love increases, all limiting factors will be removed from your life.'

At that moment, an unexpected island-wide power cut broke the circuit and the rack torsion decreased sufficiently for Kwipstah's armpits to relax. As he came to, he was filled with such a feeling of unconditional love for all humanity, that Quimper, being of noble blood, realized she was in the presence of a holy man. She undid the clasps and set him free, detaining him only long enough to sign a confidentiality clause.

Kwipstah, filled with the power of the spirit and listening to his inner voices, wasted no time in taking the next ferry over to Tenerife to catch the first flight out to Aberdeen in order, as he was 'shown' it, to prepare the people there for the second coming of the messiah, leaving Frondondo with nothing else to do but wander along to the next finca down the mountainside to discover the source of all the screaming and squealing she'd been hearing all night long.

On finding an unexpected mass of writhing bodies lost in the throes of group sexual ecstasy on the cool flagstone finca floor, she hesitated only long enough to wipe the dust from her riding crop and remove the clips from her tightly pulled-back hair, before jumping into the teeming throng to contribute what she could.

At those times when you feel constricted by the situation you're in, remember all restrictions are first created in the mind. To remove all constriction now, affirm with gusto: 'I now remove all self-imposed constrictions in my life and allow the mystery to unfold without limitation.'

64

Sitting in Klekenko's Tenerife beachfront bar after attempting unsuccessfully to purchase a small timeshare villa, Snopme Chaddelow, one-time head of the largest private security firm in all Argentina before being busted for financing a big acid haul, looked up from his vodka and was surprised to see the snappily dressed psychic tarot reader from his home town of Brighton on the UK's south coast – the one who'd advised him to look for a Tenerife timeshare in the first place – sitting with a silver-haired man who seemed to be in quite some pain from what looked like a broken hand, talking frantically on a mobile phone while another younger man hovered eagerly by.

Not having anything better to do, he sauntered over. Rivero Sambation casually unbuttoned his summer-weight Richard James-style suit that accentuated his good bits and hid the bad and explained how he'd been sent here to cover a power yoga story on the nearby semi-arid desert island of Gomera, as editor for a new glossy lifestyle magazine published by his one-time childhood bisexual lover, beret-sporting Glednel Jiltch, the nuclear terrorist who'd finally achieved a lifetime's ambition to become a big global media player. Sambation introduced the silver-haired man with broken knuckles as Harvard Arequipa, lawyer for the estate of notorious underworld figure, the late Rits Historìco, here, also on his advice, to look for a woman who'd made off with six million of his dead client's Swiss francs, and whom they believed had, as it happened, just escaped through the toilet window.

He then introduced the other younger man, Swink Taloon, up-and-coming experimental breaks DJ, fresh out of Southend-on-Sea, also a client of Arequipa, who'd tracked him down here through his office because he urgently needed Harvard to get his advance from the record company for his new mix album, which Arequipa was now attending to via the mobile phone lodged in the crook of his neck.

All at once, information overload combined with the swirl of recent events was compounded by vodka, causing Chaddelow's head to spin as he keeled over onto Arequipa's broken knuckles, eliciting a roar of such deafening proportions his eardrums burst. In the midst of that searing pain, appeared a being, (maybe an angel, maybe a barefoot doctor), who said, 'Snopme, oh, Snopme, maybe it's time to take up meditation. It'll help slow you down. It'll help you listen to the true wisdom that comes from that silent place deep inside,' and disappeared. But Snopme didn't hear a single word because his eardrums had burst.

If the world's noise is causing your head to spin, stop, sit comfortably, and half close your eyes. Focus on your breathing. Slow down the tempo of your inhalation and exhalation. Count nine breath cycles, all the while breathing in tranquility and breathing out all the noise.

65

Klekenko Wallis, one-time suburban housewife turned supermodel then internet start-up company paper billionaire, and no ordinary girl, who'd indulged her lifelong desire to open a beachfront bar and had finally settled on one in Tenerife, which she'd named Klekenko's, in honour of her great grandfather Klekenko, had arrived emotionally and hormonally at that stage of life when one needs either to open an international chain of organic fast-food restaurants or start a family.

Nuclear terrorist and glossy lifestyle magazine publisher, beret-sporting Glednel Jiltch, had been making increasingly intense overtures of late, showering her with luxury holidays, expensive jewels and exclusive Parisian perfumes in an effort to win her hand, and though she was flattered by the attention, even courted it at times, it only seemed to serve to push her further the other way.

Eventually her mind was made up, and without wasting a moment she proceeded to roll out her retail operation, opening three units a week in the UK and Netherlands, eventually spreading as far afield as Tokyo and even taking a flyer on a flagship restaurant in Western Samoa, mostly for the publicity angle. She felt she couldn't rest until the entire globe had easy access to mid-priced organic fast food.

In a last-ditch attempt to woo her, at length Glednel persuaded her to spend an evening with him in front of the log fire in his St Moritz chalet, during which he plied her remorselessly with pills, cocaine and champagne until both were gushing and gurgling on uncontrollably about love, marriage and children in an unrealistically sentimental way, to the extent that Wallis's eyes started flickering so wildly she entered a profoundly altered state of consciousness, out of the depths of which a being materialized, (maybe an angel, maybe a barefoot doctor), who said, 'Don't feel obliged to live anyone else's dream, Klekenko, especially his. Jiltch may be a charmer, but he's harbouring a lot of suppressed childhood rage. He's a loose cannon waiting to go off. Maybe you'd be better off devoting your creative energies to rolling out your marketing strategy and leave child-rearing to more earthmothery types.'

Klekenko was quite taken aback by the being's pragmatic forthrightness and was just about to gurgle something in response when she realized he'd already disappeared.

Carefully she collected her belongings and, calling for a horse-drawn sleigh on her mobile, wasted no time in catching the first flight back to Frankfurt to work on her plans.

Sometimes when you're faced with choice, you need to swing with your fascination all the way in one direction just to swing all the way back in the other. In time the pendulum will come to rest at a state of equilibrium. Take a deep breath and as you exhale, as if talking to the entire universe, declare, simply: 'I surrender!'

66

When one-time solar-architect and Goa trance DJ, Daveyroll Dùsh, on a mission to relax, walked with retro-flares flapping into the mountainside finca on the semi-arid desert island of Gomera, where Placentia Ordanato, the ravishing beauty who used to hold all New York and London in the palm of her hand, was purportedly teaching a power yoga retreat, and was greeted by the sight of a mass of writhing bodies lost in the throes of group sexual ecstasy on the cool flagstone finca floor, it disturbed him deeply. He'd seen too many kids go over the top and lose their minds in drug-fuelled orgies in Goa.

Not even stopping to introduce himself, he jumped straight back into the waiting cab and made directly for the port to catch the next ferry back to Tenerife, where he wandered into the near-est hair salon to have his head shaved and his moustaches waxed, as he always did at times of great existential stress.

When Uttlu Rormatage, who'd lost everything in an Australian divorce, taken an intensive hair-dressing training course and gone on to live out his secret life's ambition to open up a beachfront hair salon in Tenerife, saw Daveyroll walk in, he could tell this was a man under stress.

What he didn't count on was Dùsh's latent violent tendencies. These were suddenly, unexpect-edly unleashed when he applied a wintergreen wax compound to Dùsh's moustaches, unaware that Daveyroll had always detested that smell on account of an unresolved childhood incident involving an elderly matron at boarding school, causing him to spring up from the barber's chair and floor Uttlu with one well-executed chop to the neck.

Falling back into a display of overpriced luxury hair products, Rormatage lost consciousness. As slimy white conditioner from a burst container trickled down his cheek, a being appeared, (maybe an angel, maybe a barefoot doctor), who said, 'You've suffered a lot of set-backs in your life Uttlu. Don't let this one prevent you from living out your life's dream to be a great hairdresser. Even though you are about to lose all use of your hands on account of the neck injury you've just sustained, you can still be the greatest hairdresser in all Tenerife.'

When Rormatage awoke, the being was gone and so was Daveyroll, who'd wisely made himself scarce to avoid police trouble.

Wasting no time indulging in self-pity, Uttlu painfully took himself off immediately to an occupational therapist at the surprisingly well-equipped local hospital. Within a matter of months he was attracting the attention of the world's press with the masterful cuts and perms he was achieving with his bare feet and was soon doing all the big shoots for every glossy magazine in London, New York and Milan.

When you've suffered an apparent set-back, waste as little time as you can indulging in self-pity. Instead, look immediately for the new opportunity that always accompanies a crisis and jump straight into exploiting it.

67

When Bleckstrak Nengervan, one-time successful northern club promoter and recruitment consultant turned Bugis pirate dishwasher, now following his spiritual self by attending a power yoga retreat taught by Placentia Ordanato, the ravishing beauty who once held all New York and London in the palm of her hand, walked into the mountainside finca being used as the venue for the retreat and saw the mass of writhing human flesh caught in the throes of sexual ecstasy on the cool flagstone finca floor, it shocked him.

It wasn't that he hadn't been exposed to wild goings on in the past, but his emotional and physical wounds from a recent shipwreck were still too fresh for him to feel internally free enough to immerse himself in such activities, and in any case he was feeling too unsure about his sexual potency to free himself from a lifetime of

Calvinistically-inclined inhibitions enough to truly let himself go.

However, before he'd had time to turn around and shout after the cab to wait, someone in the throng, which by now had become craven for new flesh of any kind, had grabbed his ankle and pulled him into the mix.

As his clothes were ripped from his body, confused because he was sure power yoga involved more standing postures than this, Nengervan's soul did an aerial backflip and standing outside himself, now a detached onlooker, he noticed a being, (maybe an angel, maybe a barefoot doctor), who called over from across the lobby, 'Fine old conundrum, isn't it? Sometimes true peace can be more easily achieved in the midst of busy urban life than in these so-called spiritual retreats. The key, Nengervan, is service. Serve the divine by serving your fellow humans.'

While Bleckstrak was musing over this, his soul flipped back into his body and all at once he saw his path clearly before him.

Noticing that not one person was assuming the role of slave in this group, he reached out for a ball and chain someone had left nearby and asked in a voice loud enough to penetrate the cacophony of moans, groans, grunts and squeals, whether anyone needed their shoes polished.

At those times you feel excluded from the group by your own inadequacies, affirm: 'By serving the divine in my fellow humans, all my needs are met.'

68

Placentia Ordanato, ravishing beauty who used to hold all New York and London in the palm of her hand, now running – to all intents and purposes – a power yoga retreat in a mountainside finca on the semi-arid desert island of Gomera, that had degenerated mysteriously into a spontaneous orgy on the cool flagstone finca floor before the retreat had had time to kick off for real, thought she was having a deja vu when one of the participants asked in a voice loud enough to carry over the din whether anyone needed their shoes polished. She was sure there'd already been one slave polishing shoes. 'Oh, what the hell,' she mused, 'I must be hearing things.'

Suddenly, the tumult of internal noise took its toll on her, and removing various body parts from her intimate space, she got up and wandered naked outside. Whether it was from post multi-orgasmic fatigue, or from the sharply clear air, she wasn't sure but she thought she was hallucinating when a being appeared out of the ether, (maybe an angel, maybe a barefoot doctor), who said, 'Ordanato, baby, you who used to hold all of New York and Paris in the palm of your hand ...'

'New York and London,' she interjected.

'Whatever. But maybe all this power yoga business is stimulating energies too powerful for you to control. It's time to detach from the pleasures of the senses. Time to be silent inside then external stillness will surround you.'

'You reckon?' she asked, but the being simply tapped her on the throat and vanished, leaving her talking to the air.

'OK. It's time to start the yoga,' was all she said as she walked back into the finca lobby, but something in her voice seemed to stir the baser animal passions of one of the men, who pulled her sharply to the floor, accidentally catching her windpipe with his knee and rendering her completely speechless.

Often it's not necessary to go to extreme lengths to quieten the internal chatter that can block your enlightenment. Simply withdraw your consciousness to the centre of your brain, back behind the place where all the chatter occurs, and be silent inside.

69

When beret-sporting nuclear terrorist Glednel Jiltch – who having achieved his secret lifetime's ambition to be a big global media player by starting up a glossy lifestyle magazine in both hard copy and electronic formats, and now feeling it time to start a family, had latched on romantically to Klekenko Wallis, one-time suburban housewife and no ordinary girl, who'd eschewed a lucrative modelling contract to pursue her lifelong dream of owning an internet start-up company, which did so well in spite of market trends she bought a Tenerife beachfront bar she'd named Klekenko's and was also in the process of a global roll-out of a chain of organic fast-food restaurants – was finally jilted by Klekenko in favour of her career, he was not a happy boy.

Jiltch's jilting, which reawoke in him the ancient childhood memories of abandonment that subliminally had all along been the root cause of his nuclear terrorism tendencies, now stirred his deepest, most violent passions.

Feeling impotent, he decided to strike out in the only way he knew. Opening the detonation programme on his laptop, he scanned the world map and decided on Geneva, city of peace, watch-making and cheese fondue, as being the most appropriate target for a bit of a nuclear splash. He was just about to press 'enter' when his hand was stayed by what appeared to be a being (maybe an angel, maybe a barefoot doctor), who said, 'It would be far less messy if you could process that suppressed internal rage, by, say, visiting a compe-tent psychotherapist or taking up squash. Think again before making a big move like this, Glednell,' at which the being vanished, thought-lessly dropping Glednell's hand so clumsily that it hit the mouse, which scrolled down the 'g's' for a few lines, then bounced off onto the 'enter' com-mand, thus releasing a state-of-the-art nuclear-tipped medium-range missile targeted directly at the semi-arid desert island of Gomera.

If, through feelings of impotence, you feel like lashing out at others, stop for one moment and take a deep breath. As you exhale, affirm: 'I am filled with all the power that ever was, ever is and ever will be.' If after that you still feel like nuking some city or other, go right ahead, I guess; but don't blame me when the cops come looking for you.

70

As Dallalia Wilkins – petite one-time New Age con artiste turned aromatherapy healer, who having found six million Swiss francs in an expensive Italian attaché case under a parked car in New Mexico, and through wise investments having ended up as a top Broadway producer, but was now on the run from Harvard Arequipa, lawyer to the estate of notorious underworld figure, the late Rits Historìco, on a mission to retrieve his client's money – bolted down the back streets of Tenerife, she had to think fast on her feet.

She had to get off the island. After ascertaining on her mobile cellphone that the last flight out had already boarded ready for take-off, she made a beeline for the harbour, and approaching the first ostentatious tourist with a speedboat she came to, offered him €500 to take her over to the nearby semi-arid desert island of Gomera, where she was somehow sure she'd be safe.

Unbeknownst to her, however, Arequipa, in the company of Rivero Sambation, one-time psychic tarot reader, now glossy lifestyle magazine editor, and Swink Taloon, up-and-coming experimental beats DJ, was, on account of Sambation's advanced telepathic faculties, hot in pursuit.

Alighting from the speedboat and feeling herself drawn in a north-westerly direction, Dallalia followed her nose over high hill and deep dale, and eventually arrived at the mountainside finca where Placentia Ordanato, ravishing beauty who used to hold all New York and London in the palm of her hand, but who was now temporarily mute, was attempting to teach a power yoga retreat which had unexpectedly spontaneously erupted into a fully-fledged orgy on the cool flagstone finca lobby floor. Dallalia walked in to the sight of a mass of writhing bodies all lost in the throes of group sexual ecstasy – apart from one young man polishing shoes on the narrow staircase – followed closely at heel by Arequipa, Sambation and Swink, at the precise moment an unexpected guided nuclear-tipped missile impacted erroneously on Gomera, transforming it instantaneously from semi-arid to fully-blown (arid).

In that moment a being, (maybe an angel,

maybe a barefoot doctor), appeared to them all simultaneously and said, 'This is the big one, my friends – the final frontier. From here, if you stay focused on the light, you will be led to full redemption and will no longer need to take form again, but will be free to ride the winds of the nine celestial spheres, as Golden Immortals on the backs of dragons each larger than the entire Louvre in Paris, France, for eternity!'

But no one heard a word he said because they were all stone dead.

Be sure that when that still, small voice inside gives you important data which could affect you for eternity, you're not too dead inside to receive it. Affirm: 'I am always open to guidance from the highest realms of consciousness.'

From the timeless state before you were born, to the timeless state after you die, and all the way in between, while you live your life with the illusion of the progression of linear time, there resides within you a being, maybe an angel, maybe your innermost self, who watches over you, watches out from you as the action unfolds, protects you, directs you and connects you to all

*that is, the Tao. Welcome the being now and your life
will be instantly transformed into a series of miracles
(quantum events) of such magnitude that you will be
utterly surprised (and delighted).*

✦

71

Lango Faldo, one time world-famous spiritual teacher, ex-prime-time family entertainment TV presenter, personal fitness trainer and sometime timeshare salesman, now wiling away his time on Koh Samui, holding forth on matters spiritual to anyone who'd listen at a bar just north of Lamai, couldn't believe his eyes as he looked up and saw the British news on the widescreen satellite TV hanging on the wall.

'... mushroom cloud above the semi-arid desert island of Gomera in the Canary Islands ... wind blows fallout away from mass-tourist centres on Tenerife ... police say no need to evacuate ... Glednell Jiltch, media player and suspected nuclear terrorist, arrested for allegedly firing a warhead into Gomera in the Canary Isles, killing all participants at a power yoga retreat taught by Placentia Ordanato, the ravishing beauty who used to hold all of New York and London in the palm of her hand ...'

The voice of the newsreader standing in for Quimper Frondondo faded in and out with the sound of the waves crashing on the nearby beach. And there was Jiltch with his jaunty look and beret being led away by the cops!

'What's the world coming to?' Lango mused, as he nursed a glass of Scotch. Just then he was jolted from his reverie by the ringing of a cellphone in his pocket. With one eye on the screen, he watched Snopme Chaddelow being interviewed at Klekenko's beachfront bar about how he hadn't even heard the explosion on account of having burst his eardrums, then that Buddhist nun, Sister Kimbal Neosho, the one who'd gone for him up in California, who used to be that chump, Professo Expressional, was talking about the miracle of surviving the attack ...

'Wait a minute,' he thought, 'is this the alcohol talking? This is unbelievable!'

'Who is it?' he asked into the phone.

'Kwipstah, Kwipstah Tonk, I used to be in youth marketing but now I'm a spiritual teacher up in Aberdeen. Look, forgive me for interrupting you like this, but I got your number through a mutual friend, Trevylon Drummahk, who did the paint-finishing and gilding in your London flat once, I believe ...'

'Oh yes, Trevylon ...'

'Here's the thing. You've been a role model for me for quite a while now – I follow your style and teaching methods. I'm a great fan ...'

'Yes, but you know I'm not what I used to be – I got pretty burned out with all that spiritual teaching ...'

Tonk could tell Faldo was slightly drunk, 'I know, but in light of what's just happened...' Lango grunted.

'Well, it's moved me to form OAOSARNA, the Online Alliance of Souls Against Random Nuclear Attack. I've already been approached by Laborimu Spinnij, star of credible foreign arthouse movies who should have been at the power yoga retreat but missed her flight and was so moved by her lucky escape she's willing to put her name behind it. Some other clients of Trevyl n's, Ushash Renpet and Chipploe Muhunzalez, the guys who run Europe's largest mobile telecommunications net-work, are considering hosting it on their network as a free service for all cellphone customers.

Klekenko Wallis, the health food and internet tycoon, is doing free promotion in all her stores and restaurants ...'

Lango's attention was diverted to the screen again where Uttlu Rormatage was cutting someone's hair with his feet and talking into the camera about his lucky escape. Then the report switched to how a certain enterprising character from the north of England called Daveyroll Dùsh was profiting from the catastrophe by selling solar-powered anti-radiation suits ...

'And I was wondering,' continued Tonk in Lango's ear, 'seeing as you still have great sway over the way people think, whether you'd like to join us.'

But the events of the day and the scotch were beginning to take their toll and Lango's head had started to spin, faster and faster, until he fell clean off his stool and collapsed on the floor semi-unconscious.

Out of the spin appeared a being, (maybe an angel, maybe a barefoot doctor), who started gently massaging Lango's brow with his thumbs. 'Listen buddy, you can either hide away getting drunk and waste all your valuable experience, or you can get back in the game and shine your light.

The world needs you, Lango Faldo. Remember I told you once that life is just a dance of yin and yang? Well, your yang is rising again, my friend, and it's time to go out there and give it some with gusto!'

Lango felt a drilling sensation in the centre of his forehead that got stronger and stronger and suddenly his head was flooded with blinding light, the being disappeared, and he woke up with the sun shining on his eyes.

He wasted no time at all and within the hour had thrown his belongings into a cheap but sturdy sausage bag, boarded a plane and was on his way to Bangkok to catch the first available flight to Paris, where he set about immediately designing a range of premium mass-market T-shirts with 'Stop random nuclear attacks!' slogans placed creatively in distressed font on sleeves, shoulders, hems and hidden in the seams, that within no time had taken the fashion world by storm.

It was noted that even unshaven, wind-burnt Drifto Continental, formerly an alcoholic Californian divorce lawyer who'd taken a job at a leading Portsmouth-based arms manufacturer with a strong youth market following and quickly risen through the ranks to become a leading expert on the prevention of random nuclear attacks, was wearing one when he went to the White House to give the president a personal lecture on the subject.

If you've been hiding away from the world, afraid you no longer have relevance, come out of hiding now and share your light. Say proudly now, 'I am utterly relevant to my times – I now shine my light with gusto!'

72

Zank Drazdan III, one-time reluctant CIA operative, formerly assigned to spy on London until he realized he was in over his head, who went to ground till the heat had died down, following a circuitous route to a safe house in Catalunya where he settled in to write that novel he'd always had in him somewhere, and made such rapid progress that he now found himself on the very last chapter in which he was intending to tie up all loose ends so the story would hang together and make perfect sense, at least to an editor, when suddenly he was beset by an acute attack of unexpected and, for him, unprecedented writer's block.

Pacing the length of his quarters – up and down, up and down – to the point of wearing thin his trainer rubber, consternation etched deep into his mildly Central European features, he found himself entering a light trance state, wherein appeared a being, (maybe an angel, maybe a

barefoot doctor, maybe an interfering megalo-
maniac who just couldn't resist making that one
last appearance), who said, 'We've come a long
road, you and I. But let me tell you, Zank, the
ultimate stupidity consists in seeking conclusions.
Trying to tie up all the loose ends is a game for
fools. Life just isn't all neat and tidy. It's that very
messy unresolvability of it that makes it what it is.
Things don't make sense. That's the whole point.
They're not meant to make sense. They're meant
simply to be. Catch you later,' And was off into the
wide blue etheric yonder in a jiffy.

'That's it!' cried out Drazdan, suddenly bash-
ing his keys with renewed vigour and intent, writing the biggest lot of bollocks, selling it for the
hugest advance and still ending up complaining it
wasn't enough. (Authors!)

*If you ever feel your blessings just aren't enough, stop
for one moment and take a deep breath in. As you
breathe out, remember you are currently on a planet in
the midst of deepest darkest and, for all we know, hostile space, spinning on its own axis at one thousand
miles an hour, while simultaneously hurtling in orbit
around an unusually benevolent, relatively small star*

we call 'sun', at sixty-six and I kid you not, sixty-six thousand miles an hour! And if that isn't exciting enough to keep you amused, you want some pleasing! Just say 'thank you' (and everything will be alright. It will, really.)

With fondest love from one crazy being to another (you twisted son of a gun, you), x.

✦

Return of the Urban Warrior

High-Speed Spirituality for People on the Run

Barefoot Doctor takes you on a high-speed spiritual trip, with potent doses of humour and demystified Taoist philosophy, containing (almost) everything you need to know to excel in the fast and furious twenty-first century without cracking up. Includes:

- Advanced Taoist meditation and self-healing techniques for beginners and old hands alike
- Contemporary urban Taoist life skills to help you 'spiritualize' even the dullest moments and be the slickest operator on the block
- The ancient Taoist 'warrior wisdom' programme for peace, prosperity and peak performance installed into your circuitry simply through reading (this text)

The original barefoot doctors travelled the ancient Orient, healing people and lifting their spirits. This is the twenty-first century urban version.

Liberation

The Perfect Holistic Antidote to Stress, Depression and Other Unhealty States of Mind

Freedom is found within. Your shackles are your own inner struggle – your angst and anguish, your worries about money, your frustrations, your greed, your self-limiting thoughts and your fears keep you from being free. But if you're willing to take a chance, to go out on a limb and download this text onto your inner hard drive, you hold the key to liberation in your hand.

As always, Barefoot Doctor offers the full prescription: Taoist healing methods and philosophy, with an added pinch of Hinduism, Buddhism, Shamanism, Humanism and a heavy smattering of timeless Basic Commonsensism. Barefoot's remedies provide the perfect antidote to depression, deprivation, fear, loneliness, shyness, grief, grudges and all the other unhelpful mind-states life in the postmodern urban spin-cycle throws up.

Make
www.thorsonselement.com
your online sanctuary

Get online information, inspiration and
guidance to help you on the path to physical
and spiritual well-being. Drawing on the integrity
and vision of our authors and titles, and with
health advice, articles, astrology, tarot, a
meditation zone, author interviews and events
listings, www.thorsonselement.com is a great
alternative to help create space and peace
in our lives.

So if you've always wondered about practising
yoga, following an allergy-free diet, using the
tarot or getting a life coach, we can point you
in the right direction.

thorsons
element

www.thorsonselement.com